READY-TO-USE
THINKING SKILLS ACTIVITIES
FOR GRADES 4-8

READY-TO-USE
THINKING SKILLS ACTIVITIES
FOR GRADES 4–8

Fred B. Chernow

Carol Chernow

Illustrated by Kate Gartner

PARKER PUBLISHING COMPANY, INC.   WEST NYACK, NEW YORK

Library of Congress Cataloging in Publication Data

Chernow, Fred B.
  Ready-to-use thinking skills activities for
grades 4-8.

  1. Thought and thinking—Problems, exercises, etc.
2. Problem solving—Problems, exercises, etc.
3. Study, Method of—Problems, exercises, etc.
4. Activity programs in education. I. Chernow,
Carol. II. Title.
LB1590.3.C44   1986   370.15'7   85-21732

ISBN 0-13-762303-8

Printed in the United States of America

ABOUT THE AUTHORS

Fred B. Chernow, currently a middle school principal in Staten Island, New York, has been a teacher and supervisor at the primary, intermediate, and secondary levels. He has conducted in-service courses for teachers, as well as field tests and seminars for the New York City Board of Examiners. His more than twenty-five years' experience has included providing enrichment experiences for gifted children and remedial services for low-functioning students.

Carol Chernow, currently a teacher at the junior high level, has also taught elementary grades in Maryland and high school equivalency classes in New York City. She has been included in *Who's Who Among American Women*.

The Chernows are the authors of Parker's *Classroom Discipline and Control: 101 Practical Techniques*, published in 1981.

ABOUT THIS BOOK

Ready-to-Use Thinking Skills Activities for Grades 4–8 is for teachers of grades 4 to 8 who are eager to improve their students' thinking skills. Emphasizing reasoning and problem solving, this book offers a collection of activities that cover a wide variety of content areas.

Unlike other activities books that deal with only one or two subject areas, it offers ready-to-use, reproducible worksheets that teach and reinforce thinking skills. You can use these reproducible worksheets day after day, year after year, to help your students sharpen their minds and develop more efficient thinking habits.

All your students will benefit from these activities. Slower and average learners will benefit from the individual attention provided in the specific content areas, while more able students will be stimulated by the enrichment suggestions offered at the beginning of each chapter. You, the teacher, will benefit by receiving help in:

- teaching clear thinking
- making thinking activities fun
- connecting thinking and writing
- teaching problem-solving techniques

Chapter 1 offers activities for teaching problem-solving skills. Included are such skills as seeing relationships, drawing conclusions, completing analogies, and using common sense.

Chapter 2 guides your students to think while reading. Some of the skills covered are recognizing propaganda, reading between the lines, noticing details, making choices, and finding inconsistencies.

Chapter 3 helps your students think logically by learning about cause and effect, sequence of events, palindromes, poetic language, and categorization.

Chapter 4 offers activities for teaching reasoning as part of writing. Skills include deductive reasoning, selecting the correct definition, writing good titles, telling enough facts, and taking notes.

Chapter 5 deals with evaluating information in social studies. Here, your students learn how to use resource materials, solve open-ended problems, interpret charts, use graphs, and read maps.

Chapter 6 helps your students solve math problems by thinking logically. Activities include finding missing facts, solving money problems, estimating answers, applying appropriate operations, and evaluating statistical data.

Chapter 7 aids your students in organizing information, which will help them recall what they learn. Some of the skills are visualizing the whole, classifying essential data, categorizing, using mnemonics, and using context clues.

Chapter 8 helps your students to interpret scientific data by understanding differences, sampling, comparing states of matter, experimenting, and collecting.

Chapter 9 provides a selection of computer literacy activities. Skills include reasoning through truth tables, recognizing flow charts, using frequency tables, drawing analogies, and using computer keyboards.

Chapter 10 helps prepare your students to become consumers. The real-life situations in the activities cover such skills as locating hidden meanings in advertising, analyzing a menu, adjusting recipes, understanding unit pricing, and using a tax table.

Chapter 11 focuses on values. Students learn about rules, fair play, responsibility, choices, and acceptance of the differences between people.

Chapter 12 helps your students to improve their test-taking skills. These skills include recognizing word similarities, analyzing compound words, evaluating key words, relating statements to questions, and recognizing spelling problems.

Best of all, two important features are included in this book. The first is the Skills Index that will help you quickly locate all the activities for reinforcing or teaching a particular skill, such as critical thinking or decision making, as well as the appropriate grade level for each. Second, a complete Answer Key for each activity is included at the end of the book, to provide a quick reference when you wish to check the answers to any question. These special sections will help you organize class time so you can use these activities to their fullest potential.

Ready-to-Use Thinking Skills Activities for Grades 4–8 will help you teach your students to become better thinkers. Use it every day, and you'll see the results in each child you teach.

Fred B. Chernow
Carol Chernow

CONTENTS

Chapter 3: Activities for Teaching Logical Thinking in Language Arts • 39

SKILLS INDEX

COGNITIVE SKILL	ACTIVITY TITLE AND NUMBER	
visualizing words	Scrambled	2-14
predicting outcomes	I Predict . . .	3-9
moving from generalities to specifics	From General to Specific	3-15
creating palindromes	It's the Same!	3-18
telling enough	Telling Enough	4-10
categorizing	On Your Mark . . .	7-1
visualizing the whole	It's on the House!	7-3
classifying	Times, Places, People, Objects	7-5
using mnemonics	B-E-A-M	7-9
understanding unit pricing	Saving at the Meat Counter	10-3
	Shopping for Groceries	10-7
	Which Is the Better Buy?	10-9
adjusting a formula	More Cookies Are Needed!	10-6
analyzing a tax table	It's Tax Time!	10-13
applying values	Making Choices I	11-4
	Making Choices II	11-5
	What Are Your Values?	11-10

CREATIVE SKILL	ACTIVITY TITLE AND NUMBER	
reading between the lines	Read Between the Lines	2-6
predicting possible occurrences	What Might Happen?	3-10
analyzing a book report	A Book Report	3-17
writing a report	Writing a Report	4-4
writing good titles	Using Good Titles	4-11
writing a good ending	The End!	4-12
writing a good beginning	In the Beginning . . .	4-14
writing instructions	How Do I Do It?	4-15
identifying emotional language	Emotional Language	5-6
answering open-ended problems	Let's Discuss This	5-11
analyzing data	The Bermuda Triangle Mystery	8-12

INTERPRETATION SKILL	ACTIVITY TITLE AND NUMBER	
organizing job information	Keeping to the Facts	4–9
interpreting a chart	Reading a Chart	5–2
interpreting documents	In the Nineteenth Century!	5–4
interpreting a map	Reading a Map	5–5
using graphs	Reading Graphs	5–7
drawing conclusions	Reading a Poster	5–9
analyzing a cartoon	Studying a Cartoon	5–10
recognizing propaganda	Recognizing Propaganda	5–12
evaluating statistics	Such Large Numbers!	6–7
using information	Using the Information Given	6–8
visualizing the whole	It's on the House!	7–3
identifying important items	Important Facts	7–4
using context clues	Using Context Clues	7–10
following directions	Line for Line!	7–12

LOGICAL SEQUENCE SKILL	ACTIVITY TITLE AND NUMBER	
rewarding logical thinking	Be Logical	1–17
sequencing events	How Did It Happen?	3–6
	Out of Order	3–11
	Noting Sequence	3–12
	First This, Then That!	12–3
reasoning logically	What Are the Reasons?	3–8
making logical choices	Logical Pairs	3–13
knowing logical meanings	That's Not Right!	3–14
organizing in logical sequence	What's the Topic?	4–2
	Keeping to the Facts	4–9
	The Beginning, Middle, and End	7–8
outlining	Preparing an Outline	7–6
organizing findings	How Much Oxygen?	8–5
interpreting probability	What's the Probability?	9–10
putting ideas into sequence	Put Them in Order	12–2

READY-TO-USE
THINKING SKILLS ACTIVITIES
FOR GRADES 4–8

1 chapter

activities for
TEACHING PROBLEM-SOLVING SKILLS

The following activities provide a wide variety of problem-solving skills to help your students think better. Some are simple in approach, while others are more complex and require a combination of previously learned skills. For the younger or slower student, you may want to help the child work out the answers to the first few questions. For the older or brighter child, these activities can be springboards for more difficult exercises. Look at the end of the book for answer keys for every activity.

1-1 WHERE WOULD I FIND IT? requires you to review the use of the atlas, almanac, dictionary, and encyclopedia before letting the students try the activity. A brief review should do the trick.

1-2 A SENSE OF THE SOLUTION helps your students avoid giving silly answers that show no understanding of what is being asked. The students will have to *think* rather than rely on mere recall.

1-3 BE A DETECTIVE is a puzzle geared to younger readers. It gives practice in following directions as well as in thinking.

1-4 WHICH WORD? helps your students see relationships between ideas and words. For very young or slower children, you may want to begin with pictures or line drawings. After some success with these illustrations, you can move on to nouns and finally abstract meanings. Brighter students may enjoy constructing their own analogies.

1-5 SOMETHING'S MISSING requires you to do one or more sample questions with your class. Only after the students feel secure will they be able to answer the questions alone. For some of the exercises, your students will need to recall everyday objects, such as a calendar.

1-6 BE ON THE LOOKOUT! tests your students' powers of observation. Names of some countries contain familiar first names. Your students will have to notice and observe these names carefully. For younger or less able students, you may want to prepare a list of names from which they can select answers. For other students, you may need to give more than one example.

1-7 YES OR NO helps your students arrive at correct conclusions after reading a short story. For enrichment, ask your students to underline the phrase in the paragraph that supports each of their conclusions.

1-8 THE HIDDEN INSECT is a puzzle designed for younger students. It gives practice in following directions and thinking.

1-9 WHAT COMES NEXT? asks your students to look for a basic operation performed in each series of numbers. Begin by explaining what is meant by a *progression* of numbers, and have your students think of a series of numbers in which there is a logical pattern.

1-10 WATCH OUT! has your students look beyond the obvious. It helps students pay attention to such clue words as "widow" and "many."

1-11 TAKE A GUESS asks your students to do just that! Since many students usually do not like to "guesstimate" their answers first, you may have to check carefully to see that they do not do the actual computation *before* coming up with a guesstimate.

1-12 USING COMMON SENSE helps your students use common sense in answering questions.

1-13 MATHEMATICAL PATTERNS is for older, more able students. It should not be attempted by students who have not mastered activity 1-9.

1-14 NOW YOU SEE IT . . . helps your students gain practice in spatial relationships. They will need up to ten coins or discs to solve the problems.

1-15 CLUES AND CLUES helps your students reduce their thinking to a "yes" or "no" answer for each clue. You will first have to demonstrate the use of a simple box chart.

1-16 MORE CLUES is a continuation of activity 1-15 and involves more clues for the students to sort.

1-17 BE LOGICAL helps your students apply logic to solve two problems. Assist the students in preparing a three-column chart for question 2. Label each column "job," "birthplace," and "floor."

Name _____

Date _____

WHERE WOULD I FIND IT?

In your school library, you have these reference tools available for your use: an *atlas*, a *dictionary*, an *encyclopedia*, and an *almanac*. Your assignment is to decide which reference tool can most easily answer the following questions. Write the name of the reference book(s) you would use on the line after each question.

1. In what year was Abraham Lincoln born?

   _____

2. What was the name of the thirteenth president of the United States?

   _____

3. What is the meaning of the word "caboose"?

   _____

4. Where is the city of Haifa located?

   _____

5. What is the longest river in Canada?

   _____

6. Which city is farther north, New York or Tokyo?

   _____

7. How do you pronounce "queue"?

   _____

8. What is the state flower of Ohio?

   _____

9. Which team won the World Series in 1982?

   _____

10. Which film won the Academy Award for "Best Picture" in 1974?

    _____

11. What is the major farm crop in Pennsylvania?

    _____

12. How do salmon fertilize their eggs?

    _____

Name _____

Date _____

A SENSE OF THE SOLUTION

By thinking carefully first, before answering a question, you can avoid silly answers!
Read this short paragraph and then think about *sensible* answers to the questions below.
After each question, circle the answer that makes sense.

> Carlos is nine years old. He lives in an apartment house in a big city. The apartment is small.

1. How many blocks does Carlos walk to school?   4   40   140

2. How much does he spend for the school lunch?   5¢   50¢ $1.50

3. How many children are in his class?   13   30   130

4. How old is Carlos' younger sister?   7   17   70

5. How many pets does he have?   2   12   20

6. How many friends come to his home to play?   3   13   30

7. How many rooms are in Carlos' apartment?   4   8   12

8. How many hours does Carlos spend sleeping each night?   9   14   20

9. How many minutes does Carlos spend in school each day?   30   300   3000

10. Carlos is probably in which grade in school?   2   4   6

© 1986 by Parker Publishing Company, Inc.

Name _____

Date _____

BE A DETECTIVE

Here is a puzzle that will test your ability to organize clues. You are a detective who must find a missing child. The child's parents receive eight ransom letters giving clues. Each clue is one letter of a three-word message.

   Read each clue below and decide what the letter is. Then, write the letter on the line in front of the clue. If you are correct, the letters will spell a three-word message to tell you where to find the child, safe and sound.

_____ 1. It appears in "east," but not in "west."

_____ 2. It appears in "west," but not in "swell."

_____ 3. It appears in "batch," but not in "bachelor."

_____ 4. It appears in "father," but not in "falter."

_____ 5. It appears in "bathe," but not in "bath."

_____ 6. It appears in "zebra," but not in "break."

_____ 7. It appears in "groom," but not in "grumble."

_____ 8. It appears in "broad," but not in "bread."

Name _____

Date _____

WHICH WORD?

Because relationships exist between words, read each sentence below and figure out the relationship between the underlined words. Complete the comparison (called an analogy) using a word from the Word List. **Note:** There are more words in the Word List than you need. Some of the words are similar in meaning, so choose the precise word.

```
                        WORD LIST
    carry       less           monthly
    sentry      pedestrian     annual
    least       spectacle      biweekly
    pedestal    century        doctor
    spectator   duplicate      pediatrician
    vehicle     car
```

1. *Always* is to *never* as *more* is to _____.

2. *Dime* is to *dollar* as *decade* is to _____.

3. *Saw* is to *cut* as *stretcher* is to _____.

4. *Riding* is to *walking* as *motorist* is to _____.

5. *Hear* is to *racket* as *view* is to _____.

6. *Cruel* is to *brutal* as *viewer* is to _____.

7. *Autograph* is to *signature* as *copy* is to _____.

8. *Solo* is to *duet* as *weekly* is to _____.

9. *Scientist* is to *chemist* as *doctor* is to _____.

10. *Pine* is to *tree* as *train* is to _____.

Name _____

Date _____

SOMETHING'S MISSING

When asked to supply missing data, you must first evaluate the information given to see what the relationship or sequence is. Read each series below and decide, logically, what information is missing. Then fill in the blanks.

Hint: In some cases, you will need to call on your powers of observation. Think for a moment. Try to recall data you have observed on a calendar, typewriter, or color chart. These observations will help you solve *c, d, h, i,* and *j.*

a. 1   2   4   8   ___   ___   64

b. 1   2   4   7   ___   ___   22

c. S   M   T   W   ___   ___   S

d. O   T   T   F   F   ___   ___   E

e. 1   4   9   16   ___   ___   49

f. 1   3/4   5/7   7/10   ___   ___   13/19

g. I   VI   XV   LX   ___   ___   MD

h. J   F   M   A   ___   ___   J

i. Q   W   E   R   T   ___   ___   I   O   P

j. V   I   B   G   ___   ___   R

Name _____

Date _____

BE ON THE LOOKOUT!

How carefully do you look at words or names? Check your skills of observation by completing these problems.

1. The names of some countries include a boy's or girl's name. For example, the letters in the name DON are a part of INDONESIA, a country's name. Find the names of countries in which the following personal names appear. *Remember:* The personal names can appear at the beginning, middle, or end of the countries' names.

   ADA _____   MARK _____

   STAN _____   KEN _____

   DAN _____   TINA _____

   RAE _____   FRAN _____

   GARY _____   PHILIP _____

2. Some words have uncommon endings. The following list will contain five-letter words with unusual endings. The first two letters are missing from each one. Can you supply them?

___ ___ RVA	___ ___ IEN
___ ___ MAD	___ ___ MEO
___ ___ ORD	___ ___ LIO
___ ___ REM	___ ___ LOO
___ ___ XIM	___ ___ DAR
___ ___ NOM	___ ___ JOR
___ ___ ZOR	___ ___ GHT
___ ___ PAZ	___ ___ LTZ

Name _____

Date _____

YES OR NO

Read the following paragraph. Then, read the ten statements underneath. From the facts given in the paragraph, tell whether these ten conclusions are correct. Circle "Y" for "Yes" or "N" for "No."

I live on a quiet street. My house is at the corner of Giffords Lane and Amboy Road. On Labor Day morning, I was awakened by the sound of a loud crash. When I looked out my window I saw that a large red sedan had plowed into a parked green sports car belonging to my neighbor. A few minutes later, the police arrived. I heard the officers talk to the driver. They arrested the driver of the red car for drunken driving and took him off to the county jail.

1. This happened on a spring morning.   Y   N

2. The writer was asleep at the time of the accident.   Y   N

3. The driver was in a green sports car.   Y   N

4. The writer knew who owned the parked car.   Y   N

5. The writer knew who was driving the car.   Y   N

6. The driver was probably drinking.   Y   N

7. The writer called the police.   Y   N

8. The accident took place at the corner of Giffords Lane and Amboy Road.   Y   N

9. One of the police officers drove the red car to the county jail.   Y   N

10. The driver never drove again.   Y   N

Name _____

Date _____

THE HIDDEN INSECT

If you were told that a certain letter of the alphabet appears in the word "polite" but not in the word "police," which letter would it be? That's right, it's the letter "t."

In the following sentences, organize the letters of the words to get a clue to the letter asked for each time. When you think you know the letter for each sentence, write the letter on the line in front of the sentence. If you are correct, the letters on the lines will spell the name of an insect.

_____ 1. It appears in "calf," but not in "calm."

_____ 2. It appears in "nine," but not in "neat."

_____ 3. It appears in "trays," but not in "tasty."

_____ 4. It appears in "bean," but not in "band."

_____ 5. It appears in "after," but not in "alter."

_____ 6. It appears in "place," but not in "peace."

_____ 7. It appears in "pray," but not in "rapid."

Name _____

Date _____

WHAT COMES NEXT?

In each series of numbers below, there is a logical pattern or progression. You must supply the final number in the series. **Hint:** To do this, decide the operation(s) performed in each series, such as multiplying by 2, adding 1, and so forth.

a. 9   10   8   9   7   8   ____

b. 13   26   78   312   ____

c. 8   9   11   12   14   15   17   ____

d. 13,320   2,220   444   111   ____

e. 37   42   34   39   31   ____

f. 7   28   224   896   ____

g. 32   40   47   53   58   ____

h. 14   42   49   147   154   ____

i. 29   35   47   65   ____

j. 41   52   64   75   87   98   ____

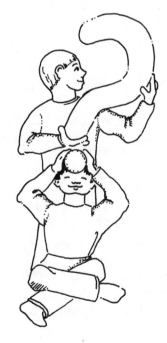

Name _____

Date _____

WATCH OUT!

Some problems can be solved when you look beyond the obvious. This is called divergent thinking. For example, how would you answer this question?

A rancher had 18 sheep. All but 11 died. How many were left?

You might want to say: (18) minus (11) equals (9.) But, if you reread the second sentence, you will see that (11) were left!
Look beyond the obvious to solve the following problems.

1. Mrs. Green visits the doctor. Mrs. Green is the doctor's sister, but the doctor is not Mrs. Greens's brother. How is this possible?

_____

2. Is it legal for a man to marry his widow's sister? _____

3. How many months have (28) days? _____

4. Do people have a July 4th in England? _____

5. Mr. White, when asked his age, replied that he was 35 years old, not counting Saturday and Sunday. What was his real age?

_____

6. If your doctor prescribed 3 pills and told you to take 1 every half-hour, how long would they last?

_____

7. Divide (40) by one-half and add (10.) What is your answer? _____

8. Find two numbers such that one is 10 times greater than the other, and the sum of the two numbers is equal to their product.

_____

9. Why can't a man living in Florida be buried west of the Mississippi River?

_____

10. A jogger walked from Here to There at an average speed of four miles per hour. He returned at an average speed of three miles per hour. If he took (21) hours in going and coming, how far is it from Here to There?

Name _____

Date _____

TAKE A GUESS

You can check your understanding of a problem's solution by taking a guess at the answer. Your answer should make sense and be based on some careful thinking.

Example: If you sit in a row of eight students and you weigh 60 pounds, guess how much all the students in your row would weigh together ($8 \times 60 = 480$). To find the *actual* answer, you would then have to know the exact weight of each of the other seven students and add the weights together.

Now try these problems. Read each problem and write your guess in the appropriate column. Then, write the actual answer in the next column.

	GUESS	ACTUAL ANSWER
1. What would be the total weight of all the students in your class? (**Hint:** Use your actual weight.)		
2. How many ounces of soda are in a case of twelve 8-ounce bottles?		
3. How many minutes in a seven-day week?		
4. How many pages in a book that is one-inch thick? (Answers will vary, depending on the book used, because paper may be thinner or thicker.)		
5. How many nickels in a collection of nickels that totals $17.05?		
6. Mr. Jones travels 19 miles each day to and from work. How many miles does he travel in a five-day week?		
7. In a class of 32 pupils, each student brought two sandwiches for the class trip. How many slices of bread were used?		
8. The teacher collected $2.40 from each pupil for the bus trip and admission to the zoo. With 32 students in the class, how much money was collected?		
9. Of the 32 students on the trip, one-half bought banners for 75 cents and the other half spent 50 cents on a souvenir. How much was spent by the class?		

Name _____

Date _____

USING COMMON SENSE

Read the descriptions of these situations and use your common sense to answer each one.

1. At a bus stop, a number of buses arrived all at once. There were two buses in front of a bus. Two buses were behind a bus, and a bus was in the middle. How many buses were there altogether?

   _____

2. What is the difference in value between six dozen and a half dozen?

   _____

3. If a quarter of forty were six, what would a third of twenty be?

   _____

4. A fish is twenty inches long. If the tail were twice as long as it is, the head and tail together would be as long as the body. The head and tail are equal in length. How long is the body?

   _____

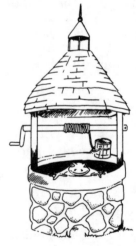

5. A frog is at the bottom of a 30-foot well. Each day it jumps up three feet, and each night it slips back two feet. How many days will it take the frog to get out of the well?

   _____

6. A blond met a brunette in the supermarket. "How are you?" asked the blonde. "Fine," answered the brunette, adding, "Do you realize your mother was my mother's only daughter?" How are the two women related?

   _____

7. Ralph has as many sisters as he has brothers. But each of his sisters has twice as many brothers as she has sisters. How many boys and girls in Ralph's family?

   _____

8. If you see a clock face reflected in a mirror and the time appears to be 2:30, what time is it really?

   _____

Name _____

Date _____

MATHEMATICAL PATTERNS

In each series of numbers below, there is a repeated pattern of operations, such as dividing by a number, adding a number, dividing by a number, adding a number, and so forth. Divide or add a number, which may remain the same or may change by increasing or decreasing in a regular pattern.

Example: 14,841   1,649   1,647   183   180   _____

What relationship exists between the first two numbers? (The second number is one-ninth of the first.) What relationship exists between the second and third numbers? (The third number is two less than the second.)

So, continue with 1,647 ÷ 9 = 183. Then 183 − 3 = 180. Then to get the answer: 180 ÷ 9 = <u>20</u>.

Hint: In some cases, you may perform just one operation (like addition) but the pattern of numbers may vary.

a. 41   82   84   252   255   _____

b. 9   27   81   243   729   _____

c. 49   147   150   50   47   141   _____

d. 49   51   54   58   60   63   _____

e. 7,783   7,777   1,111   1,106   158   154   _____

f. 83   110   98   125   114   141   _____

g. 28   28   27   54   52   156   153   _____

h. 58   65   70   78   82   91   _____

i. 2.5   25   5   50   10   100   _____

Name _____

Date _____

NOW YOU SEE IT . . .

Thinking clearly requires "seeing" relationships in space. This is sometimes called "spatial relationships." Using your awareness of these relationships, try to do the following tasks.

Remember: Read carefully and think clearly!

1. Place six coins in a row, three showing heads and three showing tails, in this order:

(H) (H) (H) (T) (T) (T)

In just three moves, with each move consisting of turning over two adjacent coins, see if you can arrange the coins so that the heads and tails alternate like this:

(H) (T) (H) (T) (H) (T)

2. Arrange ten coins or chips in the form of a triangle, like this:

Form an upside down triangle by moving just three of the coins or chips.

3. Using six coins or chips, arrange them in two columns, like this:

See if you can make a circle of coins (or chips) in only three moves. You may move only one coin (or chip) at a time, and in its new position, the coin (or chip) you move must be touching at least two other coins (or chips).

CLUES AND CLUES

You can reach logical conclusions by organizing any clues you are given. Using the helpful charts below, place checkmarks in the appropriate boxes as you come across the clues. These clues will lead to each problem's solutions.

1. Norton, Isaacs, and Allen work in a hospital. One is a nurse, another is an aide, and the third is an intern. From the following two clues, decide who has each job:

- No name begins with the same first letter of the job.
- Isaacs is NOT the aide.

	NURSE	AIDE	INTERN
Norton			
Allen			
Isaacs			

2. The last names of Ira, Julie, and Kevin are Lane, Morton, and Newman—but not in that order! Newman is Kevin's aunt. Ira's name is not Lane. Match up each person's first and last names.

	LANE	MORTON	NEWMAN
Ira			
Julie			
Kevin			

Name _____

Date _____

MORE CLUES

Sometimes, answers appear right in the problems we are trying to solve! You often just have to read carefully and organize the given information.

EXAMPLE: Ed, Ida, Joan, and Tom are two sets of twins. Tom is a month younger than Ed. Joan is a month older than Ida.
- Which pair is the younger set of twins?   Tom and Ida
- Which pair is the older set of twins?   Ed and Joan

Now try these problems:

1. John, Judy, Mary, and Roy are ten, twelve, thirteen, and fourteen years old. Mary is older than Roy and younger than Judy. John is younger than Mary and older than Roy. What is each child's age?

   John _____   Judy _____   Mary _____   Roy _____

2. A green bike, a pink bike, a white bike, and a yellow bike are all in a row. The yellow bike is not first. The pink bike is between the green bike and the white bike. The green bike is between the yellow bike and the pink bike. What is the order of the bikes?

   (1st) _____   (2nd) _____   (3rd) _____   (4th) _____

3. The favorite sports of Bob, Harry, Ivan, and Tony are baseball, hiking, ice skating, and tennis. No boy's name begins with the same letter as his favorite sport. Tony and Harry don't like team sports. Harry and Bob don't like cold weather sports. What is each boy's favorite sport?

   Bob _____   Harry _____   Ivan _____   Tony _____

4. A cat, a large dog, a goat, and a horse are named Jack, Karl, Rita, and Sally. Rita and the cat like each other. Jack and the horse go for walks together. Jack, Karl, and the goat are the largest of the four animals. What is each animal's name?

   cat _____   dog _____   goat _____   horse _____

Name _____

Date _____

BE LOGICAL

The following two logic puzzles require you to read carefully and use the information you're given. In the first puzzle, remember that *one* person can be a mother, daughter, and grandmother to three different people! In the second, you may want to use scrap paper and make a five-column chart to check off the clues.

1. Sitting around the Thanksgiving dinner table were: one great-grandfather, two grandfathers, one grandmother, three fathers, two mothers, four children, three grandchildren, one great-grandchild, one brother, three sisters, two husbands, two wives, one father-in-law, one mother-in-law, two brothers-in-law, three sisters-in-law, two uncles, three aunts, two cousins, one nephew, and two nieces. What is the smallest number of people who could have been present?

_____

2. An apartment house is occupied by five people. They all live on different floors, have different jobs, and were born in different states. From the following clues, work out the job and birthplace of each person and the floor on which he lives. Write your answers on the lines below.

   • Sal lives on the floor above the dancer.
   • The architect lives one floor above the man from Pennsylvania.
   • The person on the fourth floor was born in Florida.
   • Peter lives on the first floor.
   • Carl lives on the floor between the engineer and the man from South Dakota.
   • The person who was born in Washington lives on the fifth floor.
   • The person born in California is not an architect.
   • The baker lives on the second floor.
   • The man living on the floor between Butch and the chemist was born in Pennsylvania.
   • Fred does not live on the third floor.
   • The dancer lives on the fourth floor.

   _____

   _____

   _____

   _____

   _____

   _____

2 chapter
activities for
TEACHING READING AND THINKING

The following activities will give your students practice in thinking through the reading material they encounter. The activities include work with sentences, paragraphs, and individual words. Entire lessons can be built around them or they can be used to fill in those short time gaps that occasionally occur between lessons. Best of all, you can use the activities with individual students who need extra help or enrichment, small groups, or the entire class. Answer keys for every activity can be found at the end of the book.

2-1 THAT DOESN'T BELONG! asks your students to think of an "umbrella" word that categorizes all the other words in the series and to identify the one word in the group that does not belong. For enrichment, ask the students to make up their own series of words.

2-2 WHICH MEANING? focuses on the students' thinking of the precise meaning of a word with more than one meaning. For slower or younger students, you may want to include a Word List.

2-3 LISTEN CAREFULLY is a logical follow-up to activity 2-2. Here your students are asked to think of a word that sounds the same as another but means something different. In addition, the students must create their own sentences using the identified homonym. You might want to include a Word List for younger or less able readers.

2-4 LET'S GO TO THE MOVIES asks your students to study a movie guide before answering questions relating to the name of a film, the theater in which it plays, the times of showing, and the prices of admission.

2-5 WORD SEARCH is a good "warm up" when you want to introduce vocabulary or word-building lessons. You may want to find words with four or more letters for more able students. For slower students, you may want to supply a few more sample words, such as for, form, job, milk, or slim.

2-6 READ BETWEEN THE LINES gives the students practice in "reading between the lines." It also helps them get meaning from the printed page without going back to the text.

2-7 USE YOUR SENSES helps students distinguish among the five senses.

2-8 STEP ON A CRACK . . . gives your students practice in interpreting meaning from a paragraph.

2-9 WHAT'S IT ALL ABOUT? asks students to match twelve subjects with six book titles.

2-10 THE FIVE QUESTIONS asks students to pinpoint the who, what, where, when, and why of what they read.

2-11 FACT, OPINION, OR BOTH? helps students distinguish between fact and opinion.

2-12 DO YOU BELIEVE IT? helps students identify two forms of propaganda.

2-13 GOOD MORNING! IT'S TIME FOR BED alerts your students to be careful, thoughtful readers by finding the word that does not make sense in the sentence.

2-14 SCRAMBLED is a popular activity with many students. An additional clue appears in the phrase to help students "see" or visualize the words. For the more able reader, you can cover up the Word List before making copies of the page.

2-15 MORE OF THOSE FIVE QUESTIONS is a continuation of activity 2-10. After doing this activity, ask students to apply these same questions to their readings in social studies, science, and literature.

2-16 MORE FACTS AND OPINIONS is a continuation of Activity 2-11.

Name _____

Date _____

THAT DOESN'T BELONG!

Group names or headings tell you the kind of words that are in a particular group. You can better understand your reading if you know how to group words together. At the same time, you must also be alert to words that do *not* belong in the group.

    Look at the words in each series below. Find the group word or heading and circle it. Then, find the word that does not belong and draw a line through it.

    Example: firefighter   hose   ladder   (firehouse)   ~~chicken~~

1. clown	lion	tent	circus	easel
2. pot	pan	stove	kettle	utensil
3. kitchen	stove	refrigerator	sink	bed
4. piano	drum	horn	instrument	sign
5. pear	apple	fruit	onion	grapes
6. dad	mom	family	neighbor	sister
7. camera	lens	shutter	film	album
8. steak	chops	meat	fish	pork
9. pen	paper clip	supplies	chair	pencil
10. wing	plane	window	engine	schedule
11. sofa	lamp	living room	tub	chair
12. picnic	vacation	swimming pool	summer	snow

Name _____

Date _____

WHICH MEANING?

Many words have more than one meaning, so the precise meaning depends on how the word is used in a sentence. Think about the difference in meaning of the word "train" in these two sentences:

The *train* left on time.
Brad will *train* his dog.

In the following sentences, think of a word that is spelled the same but has a different meaning. Write the word on the blank in each sentence. The first one is done for you.

1. ____Can____ you put the ____can____ of coffee on the shelf?

2. Because of the factory _____, the boss had to _____ many workers.

3. If you _____ easily, I won't ask you to fix my flat _____.

4. Mrs. Grayson took a bottle out of the medicine _____ for her daughter's

    _____ cold.

5. In the _____, the leaves _____ off the trees.

6. Some children in the fourth _____ received a low _____ on the reading test.

7. Father tried to _____ the car near the ball _____.

8. His mind went _____ when he was asked to fill in the _____ form.

9. You have to _____ up straight if you are going to sell ice cream at the

    _____ at the school fair.

10. If you are going to _____ the meeting, you will have to bring your _____ to the front of the room.

© 1986 by Parker Publishing Company, Inc.

Name _____

Date _____

LISTEN CAREFULLY

Each sentence below contains a *homonym*. A homonym is a word that sounds like another, but is spelled differently and has another meaning. For example, OAR is a homonym for OR.

Listen to each word as you read the following sentences to yourself. Decide which word in the sentence is a homonym and underline it. Then, on the line below the sentence write your own sentence using a word that sounds the same as the one you underlined, but which has a different meaning. The first one is done for you.

1. Paul dipped his <u>oar</u> in the water.

   Grace wanted either a red or a blue pencil. _____

2. Margaret's dress was quite plain.

   _____

3. Phil and Denny took the road to the left.

   _____

4. Meat contains more calories than fish.

   _____

5. The Girl Scout troop learned about the square knot today.

   _____

6. Fish would die without water.

   _____

7. Mr. Stapleton told the class a tall tale.

   _____

8. Christopher's mother used all the flour when baking the cake.

   _____

9. Mrs. Turner's son is in the navy.

   _____

10. The mail was delivered early today.

    _____

Name _____

Date _____

LET'S GO TO THE MOVIES

Use the following "Movie Guide" to answer the questions below.

THEATER	FILM	TIMES	ADMISSION
Elm	*Space Voyager*	12 noon 8:00 P.M.	Under 12 – $1 All others – $3
Cinema	*Man Across the Pacific*	1:30 P.M. 7:00 P.M. 9:00 P.M.	All seats – $2.50
West Side	*Home on the Range*	12 noon 6:30 P.M. 8:45 P.M.	Under 12 – $1.25 All others – $3.25
Terrace	*Under the Big Top*	2:00 P.M. 6:15 P.M. 9:00 P.M.	All seats – $1.50

1. Richard can walk to the West Side Theater. Which movie is being shown this week?

   _____

2. Adam's swimming lesson is over at 1:00 P.M. Which afternoon show can he see?

   _____

3. Marie heard there is a great film about clowns being shown. Which movie should she see?

   _____

4. If Marie sees the film about clowns, how much will it cost?

   _____

5. Brian is fourteen years old and loved *Star Wars*. Which of these films is he likely to enjoy?

   _____

6. Brian plans to take his nine-year-old sister to the movie. How much money does he need?

   _____

7. Which of these films would cost the most money for children to see?

   _____

8. Where is the costly film (see question 7) playing?

   _____

Name _____

Date _____

WORD SEARCH

The following word search is made up of twenty-five letters of the alphabet, all of them except "Q." (Can you think of the reason why?) Start at any letter and, moving one letter at a time either horizontally, vertically, or diagonally, see how many words you can find.

Do not use any letter more than once in the same word. You may change direction after each letter, as in FORM.

All words must be at least three letters long, and you may not use proper names, plurals, abbreviations, or foreign words.

Try to find at least fifteen words. To help you get started, three are done for you: AIM, FED, FORM.

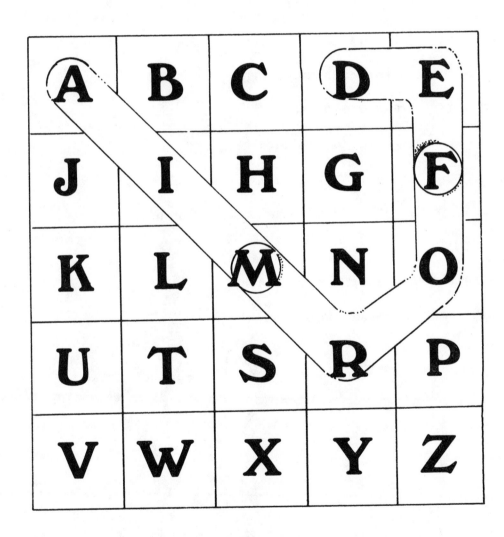

Name _____

Date _____

READ BETWEEN THE LINES

Read the following paragraph carefully. Then, fold the page so that the paragraph is covered and try to answer each question below.

There were six children. They were tired after a day of hiking with heavy backpacks. Their clothes were dusty, and their throats were dry. They headed toward the mountain hoping to reach it before sundown. One third of the group decided to turn back after the trip started. Foot blisters were their reason for dropping out. The ones who went back didn't feel the prize was worth more blisters!

. . . . (*Fold the top of this page down to this dotted line.*)

1. What kind of day was it? _____

2. In what direction were the children going? _____

3. How many children started out at first? _____

4. What did the remaining group hope to get? _____

5. What time of day was it? _____

6. What do you think the children did first at the end of the hike? _____

   _____

7. Did the children take anything along on their hike? _____

8. Were they hiking through a jungle region? _____

Name _____

Date _____

USE YOUR SENSES

Read each sentence silently and think about the images or pictures that come to mind. Each sentence describes one of the five senses:

SIGHT   HEARING   TOUCH   SMELL   TASTE

On the line under each sentence, write the sense that is described.

1. As we entered the garden, we noticed dozens of bees clinging to flowers.

   _____

2. "If I close my eyes and stand quietly for a minute, I think I am at a store's perfume counter," said Patricia.

   _____

3. As we walked closer to the bees, their buzzing filled the air around us.

   _____

4. We stared in fascination at their six legs and three-part bodies.

   _____

5. "The beekeeper placed a spoonful of honey on my tongue," said Jeremy.

   _____

6. The glossy leaves of the tall, thorny rose bush felt like leather.

   _____

7. Now it's your turn. Write a sentence of your own, following this story. Use one of the five senses and underline the sense (listed at the top of this sheet) you use.

   _____

   _____

   _____

   _____

   _____

Name _____

Date _____

STEP ON A CRACK . . .

Read the following paragraph, then read the statements below. By "reading between the lines" you should be able to draw inferences and answer each question with either "yes" or "no."

I always avoided stepping on the cracks of the sidewalks when I walked down the street with my friend and his brother. No one ever said that we shouldn't; we just didn't. One day, my younger sister purposely stepped on each crack as she ran down the street ahead of us. My friend, his brother, and I felt that our luck changed after that. It may seem strange, but we didn't win one ball game all summer after that incident. We were sure it was because of my sister's stepping on the sidewalk cracks!

_____ 1. The story has three boys in it.

_____ 2. The person telling the story is a girl.

_____ 3. The person telling the story has an older sister.

_____ 4. Everyone in the story is superstitious.

_____ 5. The people in the story live on a farm.

_____ 6. The game mentioned in the story is football.

_____ 7. The little girl accidentally stepped on the cracks.

_____ 8. The team's skill depends on whether they walk on cracks.

_____ 9. Before the sister went on the walk, the team did better.

_____ 10. It's safer for girls than boys to step on sidewalk cracks.

Name _____

Date _____

WHAT'S IT ALL ABOUT?

Look at the six book titles and their letters listed here. Then, read each sentence below and decide which book title completes the statement. Write the letter before the correct book title on the line next to each statement.

A. *Wagons West*   D. *The Final Inning*

B. *Lincoln of Illinois*   E. *The Hand in the Window*

C. *Let's Plant Vegetables*   F. *Stars and Moons*

1. _____ is a book about a famous American.

2. _____ is a mystery.

3. _____ is a book for a gardener.

4. _____ is a book in which you will find the word "telescope."

5. _____ is a book about baseball.

6. _____ is a book about pioneers.

7. _____ is a book about "Honest Abe."

8. _____ is a book that mentions horses.

9. _____ is a book in which you will learn about using rakes and spades.

10. _____ is a book that has a detective in it.

11. _____ is a book about astronomy.

12. _____ is a book about a game.

Name _____

Date _____

THE FIVE QUESTIONS

The answers to these five questions–Who? What? When? Where? Why?–help you locate details. Each sentence below contains important facts or details. Answer each question briefly.

Example: At noon, Jeff was eating lunch in the school cafeteria because his class ate during the fifth period.

WHO? ____Jeff_____

WHAT? ____was eating lunch_____

WHEN? ____at noon_____

WHERE? ___in the school cafeteria_____

WHY? ____his class ate during the fifth period___

1. On weekdays, Bob got up at seven because it took him an hour to dress and eat before getting on the school bus.

WHO? _____

WHAT? _____

WHEN? _____

WHY? _____

2. Judy delivered the *Evening Times* to the thirty-five houses in Heartland Village between five and six o'clock.

WHO? _____

WHAT? _____

WHEN? _____

WHERE? _____

3. Joan met her friends after school at Miller Field to practice before the big game.

WHO? _____

WHAT? _____

WHEN? _____

WHERE? _____

WHY? _____

FACT, OPINION, OR BOTH?

Read the following sentences carefully. Decide whether they are statements of fact (F), opinion (O), or a combination of both (C). Then, write the correct letter (F, O, or C) on the line next to the sentence. (*Hint:* A combination would be a sentence that contains both a fact *and* an opinion, as in sentence 9.)

_____ 1. Columbus reached the New World in 1492.

_____ 2. Chocolate is the best flavor for an ice cream cone.

_____ 3. According to the almanac, vanilla is the largest selling flavor of bulk ice cream in the United States.

_____ 4. Christopher Columbus died in 1506, a very unhappy man.

_____ 5. Abraham Lincoln was our greatest president.

_____ 6. Most colds are caused by wet feet.

_____ 7. Mary looks nice when she wears bright colors.

_____ 8. Lynda is nine years old and tall for her age.

_____ 9. Rhode Island is the smallest state in the United States and the most beautiful.

_____ 10. Most boys chose *Star Wars* as their favorite film.

_____ 11. Movie admission tickets cost too much.

_____ 12. Adults pay $4 on Saturday night to see a movie at the Main Street Theater.

_____ 13. Tuna fish tastes better than canned salmon.

_____ 14. Jason is the handsomest boy in the class.

_____ 15. A four-sided plane figure is called a quadrilateral.

2-12

Name _____

Date _____

DO YOU BELIEVE IT?

Much of what you read has been written to persuade you to agree or disagree with someone or some idea. This type of writing is called *propaganda*.

Careful readers recognize propaganda and avoid being influenced by it. Two popular propaganda techniques are the *bandwagon*, which asks the reader to be for or against something because many people are for or against it; and the *testimonial*, which asks the reader to be for or against something because a well-known person says it's a good idea.

Read each of the following sentences carefully. Each sentence contains one of the two propaganda techniques described above. If the sentence uses the bandwagon approach, write the letter "B" on the line. If the testimonial approach is used, write "T" on the line.

_____ 1. If Miss America is for it, you know it must be fashionable.

_____ 2. Why be different? Use Acme Soap. It's good for your skin.

_____ 3. Stan Jones of the Warriors uses a Rustee Razor. What about you?

_____ 4. Be part of the "in" crowd. Wear Gene Jeans.

_____ 5. If Marty Mall drives a Cameo, you know it's special!

_____ 6. Would Uncle Steve kid you? Of course not. I've got the best deal in town.

_____ 7. Don't be the last kid on your block to get a Fuse Computer Game!

_____ 8. Pop Poppies are good for breakfast. Phyllis Maxwell, the tennis star, has them with milk every morning.

_____ 9. Get smart! Get started! Buy the toothpaste the stars use!

_____ 10. Join the crowd! Sign up now as a Gold Bank depositor.

Name _____

Date _____

GOOD MORNING! IT'S TIME FOR BED

A good reader is always alert. This is important because errors may show up in newspapers and books—even after they have been carefully read by many people! Sometimes, your reading will pick up inconsistencies in meaning, too.

Example: When my brother has his *puncture* taken, he
blinks his eyes.
(picture)

For each of the following sentences, underline the word that is incorrect. Then, on the line provided, write the correct word.

1. I enjoy fools like ice cream, fruit, and salad.

_____

2. At dawn you could see the sun setting.

_____

3. Janet has a leading rule in the class play.

_____

4. Her years of studying French and Spanish helped Margot get a job as an interrupter.

_____

5. She grew inpatient while waiting in the doctor's office.

_____

6. It is noon and the moon is directly overhead.

_____

7. It was a clear, gray, overcast June day.

_____

8. At 3 p.m., the students departed for school.

_____

9. When the clock struck thee, the bell rang.

_____

10. We could see from her smile and twinkling eyes that she was displeased.

_____

Name _____

Date _____

SCRAMBLED

Have you ever noticed how some words appear to "jump out" at you even if their letters are scrambled?

Here are some simple phrases. Look at each phrase while trying to visualize a single word made up of each letter in that phrase. The phrases either define or relate to the word in some way. The word may even mean the opposite of the phrase, as in ILL FED = FILLED.

Choose your answers from the Word List. The first one is done for you.

WORD LIST	
FAMILIES	INFECTION
UPHOLSTERERS	LEGISLATION
HUSTLERS	PUNISHMENT
MISFORTUNE	VIOLENCE
WAITRESS	STEAMINESS

1. FINE TONIC _____ INFECTION _____

2. IT'S MORE FUN _____

3. SEEN AS MIST _____

4. LET'S RUSH _____

5. A STEW, SIR? _____

6. NINE THUMPS _____

7. NICE LOVE _____

8. IS IT LEGAL? NO _____

9. LIFE'S AIM _____

10. RESTORE PLUSH _____

Name _____

Date _____

MORE OF THOSE FIVE QUESTIONS

The answers to the five questions—Who? What? When? Where? Why—help you locate details. Each sentence below contains small but important facts or details. Read each one and then write your answers in as few words as possible.

Example: Mrs. Chase left her house on Main Street at 7:30 A.M. each morning in order to arrive at work on time.

WHO? _____ Mrs. Chase _____

WHAT? _____ left her house _____

WHERE? _____ on Main Street _____

WHEN? _____ 7:30 A.M. _____

WHY? _____ to arrive at work on time _____

1. The class trip to the museum took place on Wednesday at 10 A.M.

WHO? _____

WHAT? _____

WHEN? _____

WHERE? _____

2. Tom always watched the seven o'clock news on Channel 4.

WHO? _____

WHAT? _____

WHEN? _____

WHERE? _____

3. On Thursdays, Maggie's mother usually made a meat loaf for dinner.

WHO? _____

WHAT? _____

WHEN? _____

WHY? _____

Name _____

Date _____

MORE FACTS AND OPINIONS

Read the following sentences carefully. Decide whether they are statements of fact (F), opinion (O), or a combination of both (C), and write the correct letter (F, O, or C) on the line next to the sentence.

_____ 1. Fat people are all very cheerful.

_____ 2. History tells us about the past.

_____ 3. Juice is more healthful than soda.

_____ 4. Female workers are more dependable than male workers.

_____ 5. Not all birds can fly.

_____ 6. Zebras have coats of two colors.

_____ 7. Libraries are more interesting than museums.

_____ 8. John has long legs and must be a basketball player.

_____ 9. Jane lives on Cherry Street and must be very poor.

_____ 10. Aluminum bikes weigh less than bikes with steel frames.

3 chapter

activities for
TEACHING LOGICAL THINKING IN LANGUAGE ARTS

The following activities help your students gain skill and confidence in using language and logic. They reinforce writing skills while they give students training in using logic to think clearly. Answer keys for every activity in the section can be found at the end of the book.

3-1 LET'S CATEGORIZE helps your students group items. You may want to read the first two questions aloud and review the answers to get them started (A bear is not a member of the cat family; Wings are not found on fish).

3-2 CLASSIFYING INFORMATION helps your students classify information. Point out that several entries may be classified correctly under two categories.

3-3 THIS CAUSED THAT discusses cause and effect. Be sure your students read all the statements before they begin the activity. Prepare younger students by shutting off the room's lights. Point out that even such a simple action has certain consequences. Go on to illustrate the cause and effect of shutting off the lights. For older students, have them prepare their own list of sentences for Column B and then match them with the existing Column A.

3-4 WHY? also discusses cause and effect. Have the students set up the sentences in column form.

3-5 IN WHICH AISLE? asks your students to classify information.

3-6 HOW DID IT HAPPEN? reviews sequential occurrence. The students are asked to number a group of sentences in the order in which they think the events took place.

3-7 READ THE NEWSPAPER helps your students classify information.

3-8 WHAT ARE THE REASONS? guides your students in "reading between the lines." Students must think logically in order to answer the questions.

3-9 I PREDICT . . . gives students practice in making use of given information. They must predict outcomes and complete the sentence fragments.

3-10 WHAT MIGHT HAPPEN? asks students to determine possible occurrences based on a reading passage. They must use logic to decide if the eight situations could or could not logically occur.

3-11 OUT OF ORDER asks students to find the main idea from a group of sentences that have been randomly placed in paragraph form. You can expand upon this by asking the students to write a suitable title for the paragraph.

3-12 NOTING SEQUENCE reviews sequential occurrence. For younger students, you can supply the title.

3-13 LOGICAL PAIRS asks students to see the analogy between given words.

3-14 THAT'S NOT RIGHT! challenges students to find the word in each sentence that confuses the meaning of the sentence. The Word List will help younger students. Cover the list before you make copies for older students.

3-15 FROM GENERAL TO SPECIFIC guides your students in using words that are not opposites but are actually points on a continuum.

3-16 GOOD EATING requires certain thinking skills not used before. Your pupils will need to be able to read "between the lines."

3-17 A BOOK REPORT asks students to analyze a book report written by another student.

3-18 IT'S THE SAME! presents five palindrome exercises in order of difficulty. Begin by explaining the meaning of a palindrome, which is a word, phrase, or number that is the same when read backwards or forwards, such as radar, Bob, and 212.

3-19 WALKING ON AIR helps your students depart from exact meaning to more idiomatic language as they complete the sentences.

Name _____

Date _____

LET'S CATEGORIZE

Every time you arrange things into groups such as cities, states, pets, colors, and so on, you are using the skill of "categorizing." Every time you categorize, you are classifying. To be able to classify items, you must first know which items belong together and which do not.

    First, read carefully the words in each series below to see what the four words have in common. Then underline the word in each group that does not belong there. The first one is done for you.

    Be careful: You will have to do some careful thinking as you go down the list.

1. lion   cougar   jaguar   bear
2. fins   wings   gills   scales
3. poodle   beagle   calico   husky
4. fez   cap   beret   cape
5. Asia   Africa   India   Europe
6. wasp   asp   cobra   boa
7. chair   couch   table   rocker
8. frog   toad   salamander   crocodile
9. plan   scheme   symbol   design
10. thrifty   frugal   economical   spendthrift
11. wise   silly   sensible   sane
12. wish   want   save   desire

Name _____

Date _____

CLASSIFYING INFORMATION

There is a logical order to the way in which information is grouped or classified.

Suppose you are a librarian who receives large quantities of information daily. One of your jobs is to place bits of information in one of these four files:

(C) CAREERS   (F) FINANCE   (GI) GENERAL INFORMATION   (T) TRAVEL

Read the following bits of information and decide under which category you would file each one. Then, write the correct initial (C, F, GI, or T) on the line after each bit of information. **Note:** You may be able to classify some entries in two categories.

1. a street map of London, England _____

2. a list of commonly used medical terms _____

3. the addresses of the ten largest mutual funds _____

4. an Internal Revenue Service checklist _____

5. a guide to real estate sales positions _____

6. a pamphlet describing opportunities in the U.S. Navy _____

7. a Paris, France, subway map _____

8. a list of banks with free checking accounts _____

9. a chart of foreign money conversions _____

10. a comparison of the three most popular encyclopedias _____

11. an English–Spanish dictionary _____

12. an aptitude test for prospective computer programmers _____

THIS CAUSED THAT

Read each statement carefully. If it describes a cause, write a "C" on the line in front of it. If it describes an effect, write an "E" on the line. Then, draw a line joining each cause to its effect. The first one is done for you.

COLUMN A

__E__ The burglar alarm went off.

_____ Lucy pressed the "Play" button.

_____ Terry was home with a virus infection.

_____ They made their own wallpaper paste.

_____ The baby fell into the pool.

_____ Horse-drawn carriages began to disappear.

_____ Mrs. Gleason turned the page on the wall calendar.

_____ The elevator came to the third floor.

COLUMN B

_____ The attendance teacher called Terry's parents.

_____ Phil jumped into the water with his clothes on.

_____ The tape recorder played disco music.

_____ The Model T Ford became a popular car.

__C__ When the system is turned on, the opening of a door or window sets off the alarm.

_____ They mixed flour and water in the kitchen.

_____ John pressed the "Down" button.

_____ It was the first day of a new month.

Name _____

Date _____

WHY?

Read the following ten sentences. Each sentence describes a cause (why?) and an effect (what happened?). After you have read all the sentences, use the back of this sheet to list the causes and the effects in as few words as possible.

Example: Poor nutrition can result in health problems.

CAUSE	EFFECT
poor nutrition	health problems

1. Hens sit on eggs to keep them warm so that the baby birds may grow inside the eggs and eventually hatch.
2. Each year many Americans die in accidents resulting from drunken driving.
3. Some fish jump out of the water in order to capture insects.
4. Snakes have unusual tongues; they use them to pick up smells.
5. Birds have light, hollow bones and strong wing muscles that make them perfectly built for flying.
6. The three-month-old baby cries whenever she is wet or hungry.
7. The sun's light is so much stronger than the moon's that the sunlight hides the moon in daytime.
8. Rivers carry salt from land and rocks, resulting in ocean water tasting salty.
9. As a result of carelessness, Dave broke his leg while ice skating.
10. Fred collects stamps just for the fun of it.

Name _____

Date _____

IN WHICH AISLE?

A visit to the supermarket can be confusing and time consuming if you walk up and down the aisles without a plan. Read the following four food categories and write the name of one of them next to each item below. This will help you locate the particular item in the supermarket. **Note:** You may be able to classify some items in two categories.

MEAT   DAIRY   PRODUCE   BAKED GOODS

_____ lamb chops   _____ grapes

_____ doughnuts   _____ light cream

_____ bananas   _____ seeded rolls

_____ spare ribs   _____ leg of lamb

_____ strawberries   _____ muffins

_____ carrots   _____ cottage cheese

_____ mushrooms   _____ whipped topping

_____ bread sticks   _____ sliced rye bread

_____ margarine   _____ jelly roll

_____ butter   _____ eggs

Name _____

Date _____

HOW DID IT HAPPEN?

Below are four groups of four sentences each. Number each sentence "1," "2," "3," or "4" in the order in which you think the events took place. The first one in group A is done for you.

A. _____ Mrs. Greene was ready to leave for school.

_____ She went to the kitchen to prepare breakfast.

__*1*__ The teacher woke up, looked in the mirror, and washed her face.

_____ After breakfast, she dressed, put on lipstick, and combed her hair.

B. _____ Ron opened the test booklet and began to read the directions.

_____ The teacher asked the class to clear their desks.

_____ Ron began to write his first answer.

_____ Each student wrote his or her name on the cover when the desks were cleared and the booklets distributed.

C. _____ Louis watered the trench around the rose bush.

_____ Louis looked for a pink rose bush at the garden center.

_____ He mounded the soil around the bush and formed a trench.

_____ Louis dug a hole, centered the rose bush and filled the hole with new soil.

D. _____ Miriam took out the eggs, flour, sugar, and raisins.

_____ She mixed the ingredients with the electric hand mixer.

_____ Miriam searched the cookbook for her favorite cookie recipe.

_____ She placed the cookie sheet in the preheated oven.

Name _____

Date _____

READ THE NEWSPAPER

Sunday newspapers usually contain many sections and many pages, so you really have to think about where to locate a particular feature or column.

The following index tells you that this newspaper has eight major sections and specific information by page number and section.

SUNDAY SUN INDEX

World .... Section A	Home .... Section D
Nation .... Section B	Sports .... Section E
Local .... Section C	Travel .... Section F
Business ...... Section D	Leisure .... Section G

Art 3G	Gardens 4D
Book Review 4G	Movies 6G
Classified 13D	Music 8G
Crossword Puzzle 10G	Team Scores 3E
Deaths 12C	TV Listings 15G
Editorials 9D	Weather 2B

Use the above index to answer the following questions. Write the section letter and page number on the line after each question.

1. If you wanted to read about the President's speech, in which section would you look?

_____

2. What page would you look at to find out what is playing at the theater?

_____

3. Mr. Aiello wants to buy a used car. On which page would he look?

_____

4. Mary's mother is planning to take the family to Hawaii. Which section of the newspaper would help her?

_____

5. Jane wants to watch the new comedy series on TV. Which page will give her the time and channel?

_____

6. Which section would have a story about the recently elected mayor?

_____

7. What page would you turn to for last night's baseball scores?

_____

8. Mrs. Anderson would like to attend the funeral of Mr. Hertz, which will be held today. Which page will tell her the time and place?

_____

WHAT ARE THE REASONS?

By using logic you can arrive at answers that are not obvious. This is called reasoning logically.

Read the following paragraph. Then look at the five statements below. There are one or more reasons for each of the statements. Using logic, you can find these reasons in the paragraph. Write the reasons on the lines below each statement.

Jack and Jason Johnson are twins who love to play basketball. It has been their greatest interest since third grade. Every day of the year, including Christmas, they practice shooting baskets in the parking lot behind their apartment house. They have many friends at school, earn good grades, and have not missed a single day of school all year. Mrs. Johnson attends every game her sons' team plays.

1. The twins live in a warm part of the country.

   _____

   _____

2. They live in a city.

   _____

   _____

3. Jack and Jason are healthy boys.

   _____

   _____

4. Their mother is supportive of the boys' interest in basketball.

   _____

   _____

5. The twins are very popular.

   _____

   _____

I PREDICT . . .

Use the information stated in each of these sentences to predict what probably happened next. Finish each sentence on the line following it.

1 . Mr. Lewis heard a thumping sound from his right front tire. His steering wheel pulled

to the side. He realized that _____

_____

2. Main Street was closed to traffic. Red, white, and blue balloons were tied to street

lamps. We were going to have _____

_____

3. The bus arrived at the school at 9:15 A.M. Three parents came to assist the teacher.
The students carried their lunch in paper bags and went on the bus. They were

going _____

_____

4. Howard had trouble reading the small print. His mother took him to the eye doctor.

In three days he was _____

_____

5. Lucy was unhappy with her report card. Most of her grades were lower than last

time. When she got home, her mother _____

_____

6. Jane was getting dressed to go to the party with Jim. Jim was going to pick up Jane

at 6:30 P.M. At 6:15, Jane got a call from Jim. He was _____

_____

7. Frank was walking with his dog along a country road. At once, both Frank and his

dog saw the cat jump from the tree. The dog _____

_____

8. Jerry usually fed his goldfish a small amount of dried fish food in the morning. This
morning, his younger brother, Mark, fed the fish. Mark put in three times as much

food. When both boys came home from school, they found _____

_____

Name _____

Date _____

WHAT MIGHT HAPPEN?

The following story is not complete. Some of the items below the three paragraphs are possible occurrences and could have been included. Put the letter of the paragraph where each item belongs. Some of the ideas do not belong anywhere. Draw a line through them.

A. Charlie was a frisky dog. Though already seven years old, he acted like a spoiled puppy. He tried to take food out of Mrs. Blair's plate. Charlie had no one to play with him. There were no children living with Mr. and Mrs. Blair, and Charlie was left alone most of the time.

B. What a greeting the Blairs received when they returned home each day! Charlie was so glad to see them. When guests came, Charlie greeted them excitedly also. Sometimes he put his front paws up on the shoulders of the adults who came in and licked their faces.

C. In warm weather Charlie spent most of the day in the fenced yard. He usually dug holes in the lawn and buried bones that he got from food in the covered garbage can. He knew how to lift the lid and tip over the can. He was both frisky and messy.

1. The yard fence is more than three feet high. _____

2. Mrs. Blair worked as a nurse. _____

3. Charlie loved being with people. _____

4. He did not like being alone. _____

5. Most guests preferred visiting when Charlie was in the yard. _____

6. The Blairs bagged their garbage and left it at the curb. _____

7. The Blair's lawn was well kept. _____

8. Charlie was a smart dog when he wanted to be. _____

Name _____

Date _____

OUT OF ORDER

The following group of sentences do not form a logical paragraph because the order of the sentences does not make sense. Rewrite the paragraph on the lines below and on the back of this sheet if necessary without changing any of the sentences' words. When you are finished, underline the sentence that expresses the main idea of the paragraph.

They feel they need a name for their business that people will remember. Each commercial announcement will be thirty seconds long. A group of eighth graders have decided to start their own business. A local radio station has offered them a spot announcement at 10 A.M. and another one at 9 P.M. They plan to offer a variety of services. The commercial will feature one of the eighth graders. Some of them include babysitting and lawn moving.

_____

_____

_____

_____

_____

_____

_____

_____

_____

_____

_____

_____

_____

_____

NOTING SEQUENCE

The following six statements are mixed up and not in proper order. Put them in correct sequence by rewriting them on the lines provided below. Remember that the topic sentence or main idea should go on the first line. When you are finished, write your own title.

Lake Oneonta is a great place for kids in the summer.

The swimming is good and most people own a boat.

There are many cottages along the shore with many children in each family.

This makes it possible for them to water ski.

For those who don't own their own boats, there are boats for rent.

It is located just twenty miles from town.

TITLE _____

1. _____

   _____

2. _____

   _____

3. _____

   _____

4. _____

   _____

5. _____

   _____

6. _____

   _____

Name _____

Date _____

LOGICAL PAIRS

Read each pair of words carefully. Decide what relationship exists between the first two words, then choose a word that would logically match the third word.

Example: Doctor : hospital Librarian : _____
(*answer is library*)

1. Mare : horse Doe : _____

2. Chicken : rooster Duck : _____

3. Raisin : grape Prune : _____

4. Wrist : arm Nose : _____

5. Fish : scale Chicken : _____

6. Hammer : tool Coat : _____

7. Cat : kitten Lion : _____

8. Tap : strike Whisper : _____

9. Come : came Drive : _____

10. Dog : bark Bird : _____

11. Two : duet Four : _____

12. Hotel : guest Hospital : _____

13. Shovel : dig Towel : _____

14. Coal : fuel Hoe : _____

15. Stove : cook Dynamite : _____

Name _____

Date _____

THAT'S NOT RIGHT!

When something does not have any logical meaning, it is *illogical*. In each sentence below, find *one* word that confuses the meaning of the sentence. Cross it out and substitute the correct word from the Word List. Write the correct word on the line below the sentence.

```
         WORD LIST
grant          served
continued      damaged
choice         proclaimed
salute         pronounce
squirted       guilty
```

1. When given a cause, Gail always chooses vanilla ice cream.

   _____

2. The drop in temperature denied the coming of winter.

   _____

3. If you demand me just one favor, I will remember you forever.

   _____

4. The television miniseries was interrupted on the next two nights because it was a three-part drama.

   _____

5. The fire measured the clothing store so badly that it never reopened.

   _____

6. The airline flight attendant stowed the passengers' meals on little trays.

   _____

7. The army post gave the visiting general a ten-gun statute.

   _____

8. The voice coach told the actor to mutter his words slowly and carefully.

   _____

Name _____

Date _____

FROM GENERAL TO SPECIFIC

General and *specific* are not opposites. Rather, they are points on a scale. **For example:** You can get more precise by going from "mineral" to "metal" to "iron." Each time, you have refined the term another degree, but still related each term to the other.

Complete the following chart by moving from the general to the more specific. The first one is done for you.

GENERAL	SPECIFIC	MORE SPECIFIC
1. flower	rose	tea rose
2. human being	girl	_____
3. furniture	_____	coffee table
4. _____	grade level	fourth
5. living thing	_____	bee
6. book	chapter	_____
7. theater	balcony	_____
8. _____	state	city
9. money	_____	quarter
10. encyclopedia	volume	_____
11. _____	sofa	cushion
12. school	_____	language arts
13. building	_____	living room
14. pet	mammal	_____
15. _____	sentence	word

Now try to write one of your own:

16. _____   _____   _____

Name _____

Date _____

GOOD EATING

Read this selection silently. Then answer the eight questions. For some answers you will have to depend on what you already know.

John Otero is a body builder. He works out at the YMCA gym four days each week. His coach tells him that resting for a day between work-outs helps the body restore itself.

Breakfast is a very important meal for John. Most athletes eat their biggest meal early in the day. In this way, their bodies will perform well for the rest of the day. Some breakfast foods that provide the body with the high level of energy it needs are cereals, fruits, vegetables, and fruit juices.

Some other important foods that help build muscle tissue in the body are: meat, fish, eggs, cheese, and milk. These foods help everyone develop strength and fitness.

1. Who told John it's best to rest one day between work-outs?

   a. his doctor   b. his body   c. his coach   d. his builder

2. John probably skips

   a. rope   b. lunch   c. cake   d. chicken

3. A breakfast food suggested by this selection is

   a. bacon   b. eggs   c. potatoes   d. oranges

4. To develop strength and fitness, it's likely that John will have a portion of _____ for dinner.

   a. cheese   b. ice cream   c. french fries   d. soup

5. Body builders use similar gym equipment as those who practice

   a. boxing   b. weight lifting   c. wrestling   d. karate

6. In the month of February it is likely that John worked out

   a. 14 times   b. 16 times   c. 18 times   d. 20 times

7. All of the following are good examples of a breakfast food in the cereal group EXCEPT:

   a. corn flakes   b. cream of wheat   c. oatmeal   d. rice pudding

8. Which of these "fast food" items is probably all right for John to eat occasionally because it is relatively low in fat:

   a. cheeseburger   b. slice of pizza   c. thick shake   d. ice cream sundae

A BOOK REPORT

Read the following book report and then answer the questions below based on what you have read.

> J. L. Martin's book, *The Ocean Floor*, describes the lower depths very well. It opened a whole new world to me—a world that is full of wonder and danger.
>
> I once opened my eyes while swimming under water. This gave me a small idea of what it must be like to explore the bottom of the ocean. This book gives many facts about the ocean that I didn't know before. Did you know that a cormorant is a bird that can swim underwater to catch fish?
>
> There is a lot that is known about the world under the ocean. Everyone should read this fact-filled book. The only thing I didn't like were the many long, scientific words.
>
> > —Erin Dugan
> > Room 124

1. From this book report you know that Erin
   a. lived near the ocean
   b. enjoyed the book
   c. wants to be an oceanographer
   d. likes long, scientific words

2. Which of these statements is a fact that the reader learned from the book?
   a. Everyone should read *The Ocean Floor*
   b. The ocean is bottomless
   c. Stories about the ocean are interesting
   d. A cormorant catches fish underwater

3. The report represents the ideas and thoughts of
   a. J. L. Martin
   b. Erin Dugan
   c. people who live near the ocean
   d. the pupils in Room 124

4. Which of the following is an experience Erin had?
   a. swimming underwater
   b. walking on the ocean floor
   c. catching fish underwater
   d. writing stories about the ocean

5. Which of the following is an opinion held by Erin?
   a. The ocean floor is different from our world on land
   b. Some birds can swim underwater
   c. Much is already known about the ocean world
   d. The ocean world is full of danger and wonder

6. What didn't Erin like about the book?
   a. the dangers of the ocean floor
   b. the long, scientific words
   c. the many new facts
   d. the many descriptions

Name _____

Date _____

IT'S THE SAME!

A word, phrase, or number that is the same when read backward or forward is called a *palindrome*. Some examples are: "mom," "dad," "Madam, I'm Adam," and "1991."
    Remember, there is a logical pattern to the creation of palindromes. Try to do the following exercises:

1. List twelve three-letter palindromes, such as "nun" and "tot."

   _____   _____   _____

   _____   _____   _____

   _____   _____   _____

   _____   _____   _____

2. List six proper-name palindromes, such as "Lil" or "Bob."

   _____   _____   _____

   _____   _____   _____

3. List as many three-digit palindromes, such as "101," as you can.

   _____

   _____

4. Some dates are written in numbers. For example: June 8, 1986, can be written as 6/8/86, which is a palindrome! Try to write palindrome numerical dates for these years:

         1987   1988   1989

   _____   _____   _____

5. How many palindromic years are there in the twentieth century? Be careful and put your thinking cap on!

   _____

WALKING ON AIR

Some words or expressions should not be taken literally. For example, when you say, "After winning the game, Sally was walking on air," you do not mean that Sally was actually off the ground and walking on air! That expression, called an *idiom*, really means that Sally was "delighted or extremely happy."

Read the following sentences, paying attention to the underlined idioms. Then, look at the list of words or phrases at the bottom of the page and choose the one that is the meaning of the particular idiom. Write the meaning on the line after each sentence.

1. George escaped being hit by the car by the skin of his teeth.

   _____

2. Marie let the cat out of the bag by mentioning the party to Janet.

   _____

3. Coach Murdoch makes the girls toe the line.

   _____

4. My mother advised, "Don't cry over spilled milk."

   _____

5. The nervous salesman beats around the bush instead of answering questions.

   _____

6. Mr. Marshall's hands were tied because he didn't have a permit to fix the roof.

   _____

7. With no paycheck coming in, the Tomasi family could hardly keep their heads above water.

   _____

8. Danny's extra money burned a hole in his pocket.

   _____

was blocked	narrowly
hints at without being direct	follow orders
worry about past mistakes	avoid (money) problems
gave away the secret	disappeared quickly

4 chapter

activities for
TEACHING REASONING AS PART OF WRITING

The following activities will help your students give a logical sequence to their writing and will help them organize their own thoughts before putting them on paper, thus enabling the students to see there is a purpose to their writing. Answer keys for every activity can be found at the end of the book.

4-1 **GIVE IT A TITLE** gives students practice in seeing the connection between a paragraph and its title or headline.

4-2 **WHAT'S THE TOPIC?** guides the students in arranging sentences in a logical order so that they can find the topic sentence. Prepare your class for this exercise by reviewing what is meant by a topic sentence.

4-3 **RIDDLES, RIDDLES** helps your students develop their abilities to reason.

4-4 **WRITING A REPORT** helps the students structure their thoughts and research facts.

4-5 **THE RIGHT DEFINITION** asks students to choose the correct meaning of a word based on context clues. Students are challenged by words that have four different meanings.

4-6 **PREPARING FOR AN INTERVIEW** takes the form of a checklist. The students are to prepare for an interview with a well-known personality. Assign a particular television interview in advance of its telecast. Your students are to frame questions in preparation for the interview. When their questions, or some form of them, are asked, the students take notes. Then, they compare their interview notes in class with the other students.

4-7 **WHAT WILL I BE?** is a structured interview. Your students are encouraged to choose a relative, neighbor, or family friend and ask about career choices.

4-8 **ANSWERING YOUR OWN QUESTIONS** helps train your students in anticipating questions as they read. Your students are given practice in using the question words "how," "why," "when," and "which."

4-9 **KEEPING TO THE FACTS** helps students distinguish between fact and opinion.

4-10 **TELLING ENOUGH** asks students to "flesh out" a skeleton of a story. They are given some bare facts with which to add on additional details so that a complete picture is painted.

4-11 USING GOOD TITLES asks students to write a first paragraph to a story, given only the title. While eight titles are given, you may want the students to write only two or three. Giving them a choice stimulates more interest in the activity.

4-12 THE END! asks students to draw up a plot outline for each of the story endings.

4-13 LET'S TAKE NOTES combines two skills: note taking and writing topic sentences. Your students are to write a topic sentence for each story and to summarize the important facts.

4-14 IN THE BEGINNING . . . asks students to write one or two sentences to introduce the paragraph provided.

4-15 HOW DO I DO IT? gives students five everyday situations and asks them to write simple instructions for completing these tasks.

4-16 CONDUCTING AN INTERVIEW asks each student to pair up with another student. Each student takes a turn interviewing his or her partner on one of the two topics suggested. (It is assumed they are newspaper reporters.) Three starter questions are provided to help the students begin.

4-17 LET'S USE COMMON SENSE helps your students move from general information to more particular conclusions. Caution your students to read each problem several times before attempting a solution.

Name _____

Date _____

GIVE IT A TITLE

You really need to use sound reasoning skills when you write a headline or title for something you have written. The title must tell something about what you have written. It must also make the reader of the headline or title want to read on.

We have written three book titles and two newspaper headlines below. Your job is to write three or four sentences under each one. The title or headline will suggest what your paragraph should contain.

1. *Pecos Bill Rides a Tornado*

_____

_____

2. *The Invisible Rabbit*

_____

_____

3. *Wild Wing*

_____

_____

1. Rock Star Wows Crowded Park

_____

_____

2. Storm Closes Schools for Second Day

_____

_____

Name _____

Date _____

WHAT'S THE TOPIC?

The following sentences are in scrambled order. Find the topic sentence and arrange the rest of the sentences so that the facts follow logically.

A. She said that she was sending something for his birthday.

B. On Friday, a mail truck stopped at Ricky's house.

C. Every day Ricky watched for the mailman.

D. It had Ricky's name on it, and he hoped that what he wanted was inside.

E. On Tuesday the mailman brought Ricky a card from his grandmother.

F. A man brought a big box to the house.

G. There was a label on it: "Do NOT crush."

H. Ricky opened the box carefully.

TOPIC SENTENCE: _____

_____

_____

_____

_____

_____

_____

_____

_____

_____

_____

Name _____

Date _____

RIDDLES, RIDDLES

Before you can write logically, you have to be able to reason. You can improve your reasoning ability by applying yourself to solving these riddles. Write your answers on the line below each question.

1. What is not clothing but worn by feet? (Clue: pay attention to the word "worn.")

   _____

2. What stays hot even when it's cold?

   _____

3. What keeps things out and runs around the yard?

   _____

4. What small thing never runs out of light in the night?

   _____

5. What goes to sleep for a long time after a feast?

   _____

6. Which "toes" never wear shoes?

   _____

7. What has a bed but never sleeps?

   _____

8. What grows shorter, the longer it stands?

   _____

9. What word means "perfect" but when you subtract its first letter, it's what you do to cards?

   _____

10. What's a fruit that, without its first letter, is something you can cook on?

   _____

11. What word is the opposite of "wide"? When you take away its first letter, it points the way.

   _____

12. What is the smallest particle of an element? When you take away its first letter, it becomes a boy's name.

   _____

Name _____

Date _____

WRITING A REPORT

Assume that you have been asked to write a report on the armadillo. Begin by jotting down on a piece of paper everything you know about this animal. You may not know anything. Next, look up the word in an encyclopedia and write down in simple phrases as much information as you can gather.

After you have your raw data, put them into categories. We have given you a start by listing some broad categories for you. Organize your information under the appropriate heading. Then, write a paragraph for each category. Add a beginning and an ending and you will have an original report.

1. What does the armadillo look like? _____

_____

_____

2. What does it eat? _____

_____

3. What kind of shelter does it make? _____

_____

4. How does an armadillo protect itself? _____

_____

5. Where does it live? _____

_____

6. What is unusual about it? _____

_____

_____

_____

Name _____

Date _____

THE RIGHT DEFINITION

While a dictionary tells you the meanings, or definitions, of words, you must use your reasoning ability to choose the right definition. Some words have several different meanings. For example, what one word would fit each of these sentences?

1. She selected a red _____ to wear.

2. He _____ out of his chair when she approached.

   The answer is "rose," the same word with very different meanings. Read these groups of sentences and decide which one word can fit each blank.

A. 1. She sang in a different _____.

   2. Is this the _____ you lost?

   3. He unlocked the _____ to the puzzle..

   4. That _____ is stuck on the typewriter.

B. 1. They will _____ their concert as planned.

   2. Can you _____ me the time?

   3. _____ me one more chance.

   4. Will iced drinks _____ you a sore throat?

C. 1. The barber gave him a _____.

   2. Can you _____ the sails?

   3. She always looks neat and _____.

   4. Will he help _____ the tree?

D. 1. She was a _____ character in the play.

   2. The bar would not serve a _____.

   3. He failed one _____ subject.

   4. Play that tune in F _____.

Name _____

Date _____

PREPARING FOR AN INTERVIEW

An interview is a conversation in which one person asks questions to get information from another person. Before you can conduct an interview you must prepare for it. Organize your questions ahead of time so that your interview will go more smoothly. The time you spend reasoning or thinking before the interview will actually save time during the interview and write-up that follows.

Use this checklist to conduct an interview with a TV personality. Find an interview or talk-show broadcast in your area. Watch the TV interview with these questions in front of you. Take notes whenever one of your questions is answered. In class, compare your interview notes with others who watched the same TV interview. (You may want to use these questions to interview someone in school or at home.)

1. Where do you do your work?
2. When did you first start?
3. What kind of training or education did you have?
4. What are your long-term goals?
5. Do you have a family of your own?
6. What is a current project you are working on?
7. What advice would you give a young person starting out today?

Name _____

Date _____

WHAT WILL I BE?

One good way of collecting information about different career choices is by interviewing relatives, neighbors, and family friends. You will gather more valuable data if you structure or organize your interview.

Begin by putting the following heading on your interview sheet. (You will probably take rough notes during the interview and rewrite them later.)

Name of person interviewed:

Occupation:

Date of Interview:

Organize your interview around the questions below. You may want to conduct your own style interview and answer these questions later. Or, you may want to use some or all of these questions in conducting your interview.

1. What do you do in a typical day?
2. Which activities take up most of your time?
3. What are the average earnings of people holding jobs such as yours?
4. What do you enjoy most about your job?
5. What do you enjoy least?
6. What type of person is best suited for this work?
7. What job-related things do you expect to be doing in the future?
8. What kind of training would I need to become a _____?
9. If you were starting over, would you make the same job (career) choice?
10. What are the major problems you face in your job?
11. What have you found most helpful in meeting those problems?
12. Will there be a need for more _____ by the time I am ready?

Name _____

Date _____

ANSWERING YOUR OWN QUESTIONS

As you write you have to imagine that you are answering your reader's questions. When someone reads what you have written, he or she is silently asking questions. This is part of using reasoning or thinking skills.

Match the questions with the answers that appear in the second column. Write in the letter from Column II on the blank in Column I:

COLUMN I

1. *How* is a word that asks __G__

2. *Who* is a word that asks _____

3. *What* is a word that asks _____

4. *When* is a word that asks _____

5. *Where* is a word that asks for _____

6. *Why* is a word that asks _____

7. *Which* is a word that asks _____

COLUMN II

A. the name or description of something.

B. the time in which something happened.

C. a place or location.

D. the reason something happened.

E. the name of a person.

F. the best answer from two or more choices.

G. the way something was done.

These phrases can be summarized into one or two words, listed below. Below them are the seven question words. Alongside each question word write the one answer word from this list.

way   choice   reason   person   place   time   thing

Who _____

What _____

When _____

Where _____

Which _____

Why _____

How _____

KEEPING TO THE FACTS

When writing, you will use sentences that tell things that everyone knows to be true. These are called factual sentences. Sometimes you will write sentences that tell what people feel or think. These are feelings or opinions and are not facts.

Read the following story. Each sentence is followed by a set of parentheses ( ). If the sentence you have just read is factual put a check in the parentheses. If it is *not* factual, put an "X."

I think the weather is a safe topic to bring up at a party. ( ) I mentioned that the temperature reached 90 degrees at 1 P.M. yesterday. ( ) "June is the nicest month," said Marie. ( ) "Channel 3 has the best weather report" was my reply. ( )

"I like summer more than I like winter," announced Henry. ( ) He just returned from a week at the shore. ( ) He told us it rained every day. ( ) He described how depressed he felt after a week of rain. ( ) I don't think weather is a safe topic to raise at parties. ( )

Name _____

Date _____

TELLING ENOUGH

When you put words on paper you are trying to communicate your ideas to the reader. The reader uses his or her powers of reasoning to get your message. It is important to add enough details so that your reader will be able to use reason to figure out what it is you wish to communicate.

     The following paragraphs do not give enough details. They do not tell enough. Your job is to rewrite each paragraph so that it points a complete picture, not a mere skeleton. **Hint:** Your paragraph should answer the "who," "what," "why," "how," "when" questions the reader has in his mind. Start to write on the lines at the bottom of the page and then use the back of this sheet.

1. We went to the movies. I enjoyed the film. It was funny. We got home early.
2. I was glad to get my paper. The teacher's comments pleased me. I put the paper away after reading her comments twice.
3. He was a nice enough man. I just didn't like the idea of having someone poke around in my mouth.
4. Birthday's are fun. But deciding what to buy your best friend is not easy.
5. Some of the costumes were clever. I liked the person who was dressed like Superman.

_____

_____

_____

_____

_____

_____

_____

_____

_____

_____

_____

_____

USING GOOD TITLES

A good title makes you want to read the story. It takes good reasoning skill to be able to write a good title. It should give just a hint about the story without giving the story away.

The following titles have been taken from stories you may have read. Your job is to use the title for an original story idea. Of course, you can't write the whole story here. Just write a good first paragraph that will give a hint of what *your* story is about. Do *not* try to recall the original story if you happen to recognize the title.

1. The Day After
2. Of Mice and Men
3. Shot from Space
4. The Invasion of Ants

5. A View from the Bridge
6. Boy Meets Girl
7. New at the Job
8. A Great Loss

_____

_____

_____

_____

_____

_____

_____

_____

_____

_____

_____

_____

_____

_____

_____

_____

_____

Name _____

Date _____

THE END!

The ending is an important part of every piece of writing. A good ending makes the reader feel the story is finished in a way that makes sense. It summarizes the facts in a nonfiction piece of writing.

    We have listed five endings below. For each of our final sentences, write a brief outline of the kind of story that these endings would fit.

1. So Jamie just swam away and was sad.
2. The two of them walked down the road together—full of hope for the future.
3. The jury foreman announced the verdict in a clear voice: "Not guilty."
4. The two men shook hands, and the younger man boarded the train.
5. With great pride, Nancy hung up her shingle, which read, "Nancy Middleton, M.D."

_____

_____

_____

_____

_____

_____

_____

_____

_____

_____

_____

_____

_____

_____

_____

_____

Name _____

Date _____

LET'S TAKE NOTES

One way to remember information is to take notes. This will help you in your writing. When you take notes, write only enough words to help you remember the main idea and facts.

Read each of the paragraphs below. Using the back of this sheet, write the topic sentence of each paragraph. Then, write a few words to tell the important facts.

1. There are many varieties of plants that eat insects. Some use their special leaves to trap insects. When an insect lands on the plant's leaves, the insect is eaten. These plants do not need to get their food from the soil. A popular insect-eating plant is the Venus flytrap. When a fly lands on one of the leaves, the leaf snaps shut, trapping the insect. The sundew is another such plant. It has red vines covered with a sticky liquid. At night, the vines close around the insect like arms. The pitcher plant drowns insects in a pool of its own juice.

2. One kind of Spanish music is called flamenco. It was developed by Arabian, Gypsy, and Spanish people. Flamenco is actually three kinds of music: the dance, the song, and the guitar music. The birthplace of flamenco was in a part of Spain called Andalusia. Artists like José Limón and Carmen Amaya have spread flamenco to all parts of the world.

3. Birds take care in choosing the location of their nests. In spite of this, many baby birds, as well as the nests, are lost during heavy spring storms. Most birds do not nest high in the tree. Many birds nest less than ten feet above the ground.

Name _____

Date _____

IN THE BEGINNING . . .

When you write a story you need to think of a good beginning. Your first sentence has to catch a reader's attention.

The paragraphs below have been taken from different stories. The stories need good beginnings. Read each paragraph. Then, write *one* or *two* sentences for each story that will serve as an attention-getting start. Use the lines at the bottom of this sheet and then use the back of this paper.

1. . . . I looked at myself in the full-length mirror. For a moment the glass reflected a girl I barely recognized. The gown fit beautifully. The girl in the mirror looked older and prettier than the girl I usually saw reflected.

2. . . . It was late. I was already ten minutes late by the time I sat down to eat. Perhaps I'd better skip breakfast today.

3. . . . It wasn't on my desk. I looked on the hall table. I looked everywhere but couldn't find it. What could I tell him?

4. . . . The silence was killing me. If only one of them would say something. Even if they yelled at me, I would feel better. The long, cold stares and no talking were really getting me down.

5. . . . I counted the bills in my wallet for the third time. There should have been eighteen dollars there, and I found only eight single bills. Where did the ten-dollar bill go?

_____

_____

_____

_____

_____

_____

_____

_____

_____

_____

_____

_____

Name _____

Date _____

HOW DO I DO IT?

When you write instructions for a reader to follow you need good reasoning skills. You must put the steps in the right order. The steps must be short but complete enough to give the necessary information.

Write simple instructions for these everyday activities. Each set of instructions will include five or six steps. Be sure they are in the correct order. Put the correct number next to each step in the instructions.

A. tying a pair of shoe laces

B. making a bed

C. preparing a favorite ice-cream sundae

D. teaching someone to ride a bike

E. covering a school book

_____

_____

_____

_____

_____

_____

_____

_____

_____

_____

_____

_____

Name _____

Date _____

CONDUCTING AN INTERVIEW

Below are two headlines from a daily newspaper. You are going to interview your partner for one of these stories, and your partner will interview you for the other.

"Youngest Person Ever Wins State Lottery"

"Private Pilot Survives Mountain Crash"

After the interviews, write your own newspaper story. First, decide which of you is going to be the lottery winner and which is going to be the pilot. Next, use the three starter questions we have given each of you. Finally, take down your partner's comments in note form and then write your newspaper story.

"Youngest Person Ever Wins State Lottery"

1. When and where did you buy the ticket?
2. How did you feel when you found out that you won?
3. What plans have you made for using the money?

"Private Pilot Survives Mountain Crash"

1. What are the details of the crash?
2. How did you survive?
3. How were you rescued?

Name _____

Date _____

LET'S USE COMMON SENSE

There is a ''common-sense'' approach to solving problems. You reason from information given to you. This is called deductive reasoning; you go from general information to more particular conclusions.

To solve the following problems, you will need to read each paragraph at least twice. It may also be helpful if you make some notes on scrap paper.

1. Mrs. Kress had three children: Michael, Tricia, and Bernie. She gave them each some chores to do. One was told to wash the dishes, another was told to clean the stove, and the third child was told to unpack the groceries. Each child performed the chore assigned. Michael did not wash the dishes. Tricia did not clean the stove, Bernie did not unpack the groceries nor did he clean the stove. Who did which chore?

2. Mr. A and Mr. J are fathers with both full- and part-time jobs. The four jobs are lawyer, teacher, carpenter, and computer repairman. The carpenter knows nothing about computers. Mr. A is not a teacher. Mr. J knows nothing about carpentry. Find each father's two jobs.

3. There are four boys on the Math Team: Alan, Felix, George, and Harry. Alan, Felix, and George have dark eyes. Alan, George, and Harry have brown hair. Felix and George have straight hair. Alan and Harry have curly hair. Describe each boy. One boy has blue eyes and another boy has black hair. None of the boys have curly black hair.

5 chapter

activities for EVALUATING INFORMATION IN SOCIAL STUDIES

Successful teachers have found that mere mastery of a body of factual material is not the best way to learn social studies. The learning process must involve critical thinking and the evaluation of information. Therefore, the following activities involve reason and emotion as the children learn, question, apply their value standards, and adjust their attitudes. Answer keys for every activity can be found at the end of the book.

5-1 **IT'S FOUND HERE!** reviews common reference books (atlas, almanac, dictionary, and encyclopedia) found in the classroom and school library. Go over the kinds of articles found in some popular magazines and review parts of a book, such as the table of contents, glossary, and index. For extra credit, have students look up the answers to questions 2, 3, 5, and 6.

5-2 **READING A CHART** presents social studies information in tabular form. Discuss with the students the four columns to the chart and do the first question together.

5-3 **UNFINISHED THOUGHTS** can be handled more easily by your students if it follows a lesson on pollution. In your lesson, include a discussion of the kinds of pollution (air, water, soil, and sound); the kinds of enforcement tools (fines and restraining orders); and pollution's effects (health, quality of life, wildlife, and economics).

5-4 **IN THE NINETEENTH CENTURY!** shows a document that is authentic in language and capitalization. Have students try to guess why certain words are capitalized (Interpreter—title; Brothers, Business, Mischief—key words). In question 1, it is important that the students use their own words to demonstrate their understanding.

5-5 **READING A MAP** gives important practice in map skills. This activity asks students to interpret information from a detailed map.

5-6 **EMOTIONAL LANGUAGE** helps students identify strong feeling when they read a news article. Students are alerted to watch for words or phrases that attempt to color the truth. To assist poorer readers, you may want to help them find the first emotional-language sentence.

5-7 **READING GRAPHS** shows four graphs related to the Great Depression. Guide your students in finding the answers to the eight questions by looking at the three line graphs and one bar graph.

5–8 THAT'S NOT RELEVANT helps students reach a conclusion based on facts given. Students are asked to decide which facts are relevant to a given situation. For extra credit, have some students make up a similar activity of their own to try out on the rest of the class.

5–9 READING A POSTER shows a representation of an authentic slave-sale poster. Have students read the entire poster before attempting to answer the six questions. Insist that the answers be written in complete sentences.

5–10 STUDYING A CARTOON asks your students to answer five thought-provoking questions about a 1774 cartoon. Explain that there are many different kinds of cartoons, ranging from comical to satirical to political.

5–11 LET'S DISCUSS THIS applies social studies knowledge and skills to everyday situations. Before attempting it with your students, be sure they have had practice in writing down their point of view on a subject. These real-life situations are within the experience of most of your students.

5–12 RECOGNIZING PROPAGANDA asks students to pick out propaganda that is used to make some people look good while making others look bad. Help your students relate name-calling to the kind of hurtful activity that many youngsters engage in.

IT'S FOUND HERE!

Your school library contains many reference books, magazines, and other materials. To get the most out of the library you must look for answers in the right place. Think about each of these questions before selecting your answers.

1. Where would you look in a history book to find the pages that tell about the Battle

   of Bunker Hill? _____

   a. glossary   c. table of contents

   b. preface   d. index

2. Which of these would tell you the name of the thirteenth President of the United

   States ? _____

   a. atlas   c. world almanac

   b. picture dictionary   d. *Reader's Digest*

3. Which of these would tell you whether Washington, D.C., is north of Tokyo, Japan?

   _____

   a. map of United States   c. encyclopedia

   b. map of North America   d. globe

4. Which magazine would be most likely to contain pictures of recent news events?

   _____

   a. *TV Guide*   c. *Time*

   b. *National Geographic*   d. *People*

5. Where are you most likely to find facts about the boyhood of Franklin D. Roosevelt?

   _____

   a. in a book called *Five Famous*   c. in a book called *Civil War*
      Presidents   *Presidents*

   b. in a dictionary   d. in an encyclopedia

6. If you wanted to find out the name of the longest river in Mexico you would use any

   of these *except:* _____

   a. a world almanac   c. a Spanish-English dictionary

   b. an encyclopedia   d. an atlas

Name _____

Date _____

READING A CHART

After the Constitutional Convention the thirteen states had to approve or ratify the Constitution. Read this chart to see how and when each state voted. Then, answer the questions below.

THE VOTE ON THE CONSTITUTION

State	Date	Vote for	against
Connecticut	January 9, 1788	128	40
Delaware	December 7, 1787	Unanimous	
Georgia	January 2, 1788	Unanimous	
Maryland	April 26, 1788	63	11
Massachusetts	February 6, 1788	187	168
New Hampshire	June 21, 1788	57	47
New Jersey	December 18, 1787	Unanimous	
New York	July 26, 1788	30	27
North Carolina	November 21, 1789	195	77
Pennsylvania	December 12, 1787	46	23
Rhode Island	May 29, 1790	34	32
South Carolina	May 23, 1788	149	73
Virginia	June 25, 1788	89	79

1. Which was the first state to approve or ratify?

_____

2. In which state was the vote closest?

_____

3. Which states voted unanimously for the Constitution?

_____

4. George Washington took office as President on April 30, 1789. Which two states did not ratify until after he became President?

_____

5. Which was the ninth state to ratify?

_____

Name _____

Date _____

UNFINISHED THOUGHTS

Your understanding of broad topics in social studies can be improved when you finish incomplete sentences. This activity strengthens your ability to think.

    The topic in the unfinished sentences below concerns "pollution." Think about each unfinished sentence carefully before you write in the rest of it.

1. The best way to reduce noise in my neighborhood is to

_____

2. My school grounds would look better if

_____

3. If I were mayor I would reduce pollution by

_____

4. The laws regulating pollution should be

_____

5. The newspapers should print more stories about

_____

6. Pollution would be reduced if people would

_____

7. When I was younger, I made our pollution problem worse when I

_____

8. One of the worst offenders in our town is the

_____

9. Our school could help by

_____

_____

10. By the year 2000 I think that the problem of pollution will be

_____

_____

Name _____

Date _____

IN THE NINETEENTH CENTURY!

The following is a message from the Governor of the Mississippi Territory to the Choctaw Indians.

Brothers,

I sent my Interpreter David Berry to you, on this morning, with a request that you would come and see me; but you have thought proper to decline doing so.

I will tell you Brothers my Business with you; I was informed on yesterday, that you had gone to a white Man's House, and killed one of his work Steers, wounded another, and threatened to do him further Mischief.

I wanted to have you and the white man face to face, in order, that I might learn the truth; But it seems you will not come near me.

Now Brothers, I must inform you, that I do not allow my people to treat a red man amiss, nor will I suffer a red man, to treat any of my people amiss.

I will forget and forgive your late bad Conduct, upon one Condition, which is, that you immediately depart for your own Land, and do no more mischief.

My Interpreter David Berry will bring to me, your answer to this talk.

William C. C. Claiborne

1. What problem did Governor Claiborne want to solve? (Use your own words.)

   _____

2. How did the Governor first try to learn the truth?

   _____

3. Why didn't his first plan work out?

   _____

4. Which paragraph describes his ideas on fair play?

   _____

5. How does he address the Indians? Why is this significant?

   _____

6. What skills did David Berry have?

   _____

Name _____

Date _____

READING A MAP

Study the product map of the Colonies. Then, answer these questions.

1. Using the scale of miles, decide the approximate distance in miles from the eastern to the western borders of Pennsylvania.

   _____

2. Which colony was founded first? _____
   Which two colonies were founded in 1636?

   _____

3. Which colonies made up the "breadbasket" of America?

   _____

4. Which colonies were drawn together by their interest in raising tobacco and rice?

   _____

5. Which colonies depended on the sea a great deal?

   _____

6. Estimate the distance in miles from the northern tip of New Hampshire to the southern tip of Georgia.

   _____

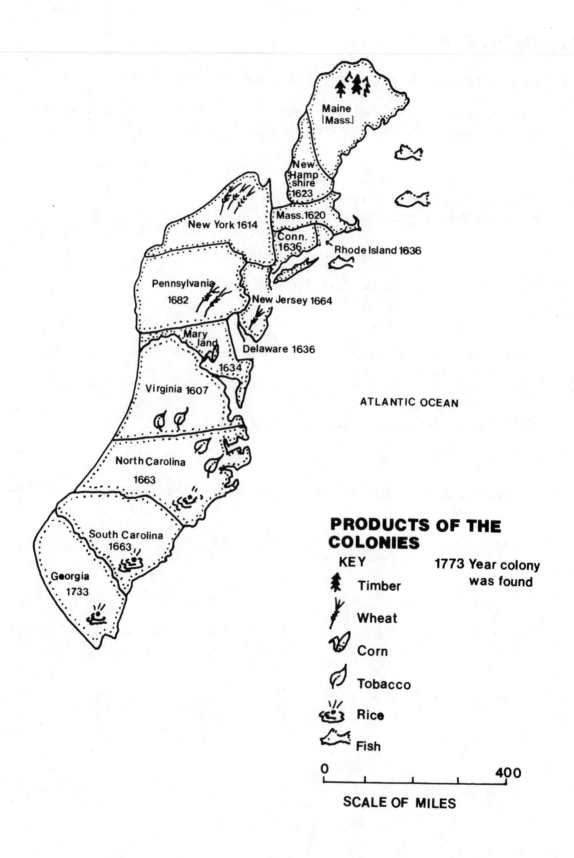

Maine
[Mass.]

New
Hamp-
shire
1623

New York 1614

Mass. 1620

Conn.
1636

Rhode Island 1636

Pennsylvania
1682

New Jersey 1664

Mary
land

Delaware 1636

1634

Virginia 1607

ATLANTIC OCEAN

North Carolina
1663

South Carolina
1663

Georgia
1733

PRODUCTS OF THE COLONIES

KEY

1773 Year colony
was found

Timber

Wheat

Corn

Tobacco

Rice

Fish

0   400

SCALE OF MILES

Name _____

Date _____

EMOTIONAL LANGUAGE

Alert readers are always on the watch for certain words or phrases that try to color the truth. Some writers try to persuade the reader by using language that is emotional, or of strong feeling.

Read the following article. Find three sentences in the article that contain at least three "emotional" words, that is, words with strong feeling. Draw a line through the "emotional" words. Rewrite these sentences without the emotional language.

Jack Cosmo, mayor of Middletown, has submitted his resignation to the City Council.

The handsome, highly successful businessman told the stunned Council that he was leaving for personal reasons. Cosmo, the forty-three-year-old former car dealer, said he was tired of fifteen-hour days. Council members close to Town Hall have heard reports that he has health problems relating to a long, losing battle with alcohol.

Those present seemed unwilling to accept Cosmo's explanation. It is widely known that when at the Cosmo Auto Agency, Jack Cosmo put in even longer hours. Under the new charter a new mayor will be selected by the recently elected full-time City Council. Their next regularly scheduled meeting is January 23rd.

Name _____

Date _____

READING GRAPHS

Look at the following four graphs. Then, read the questions and write your answers on the lines provided.

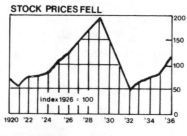

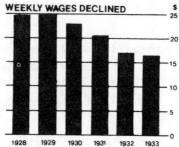

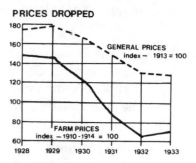

1. In what year did the stock price index reach 200?

_____

2. In 1932 unemployment reached how many million?

_____

3. Was unemployment higher in 1928 or 1929?

_____

4. Weekly wages averaged $25 in which year?

_____

5. Wages sunk to $21 in which year?

_____

6. Farm prices in 1930 were approximately how much?

_____

7. The general price index reached 130 in which year?

_____

8. Between 1929 and 1932 the stock price index fell how many points?

_____

Name _____

Date _____

THAT'S NOT RELEVANT

When you reach a conclusion based on facts given, you are using inductive thinking. The facts must be relevant. That means "having to do with," "applicable to," or "connected with."

In each of these two exercises place a check alongside the facts that are relevant. Put an "X" in front of the items that are not relevant (irrelevant).

1. Ed Cook is running for mayor. His voting record on the City Council is relevant to the question of whether or not he would be a good mayor. The fact that he has two dogs is not.

   a. _____ He is a strong leader.

   b. _____ He was a successful consumer affairs lawyer before running for the City Council.

   c. _____ He has three children.

   d. _____ All his children won college scholarships.

   e. _____ Ed was a star football player.

   f. _____ His wife was treated for an alcohol problem.

   g. _____ He is known to be extremely honest.

   h. _____ He had an excellent attendance record when on the City Council.

2. While driving a car in a foreign country your father gets lost. He stops at a farmhouse to ask directions to the next town. With your help your father is able to translate the farmer's directions. Which of these statements are relevant?

   a. _____ You'll pass a white church. That's the one we attend on Sunday.

   b. _____ You'll see a white church. Make a left turn just after the church.

   c. _____ Looks like rain. You'll have to hurry.

   d. _____ It's about 10 kilometers as the crow flies.

   e. _____ You're the second person to ask me for directions today.

   f. _____ If you see a firehouse you will know you went too far down this road.

   g. _____ You might like to buy some of my vegetables before you leave.

   h. _____ Go slowly around the curve in the road, your right turn comes after the church.

Name _____

Date _____

READING A POSTER

On the following page is a poster advertising a slave sale in 1835. Examine it carefully and then answer the questions in complete sentences.

1. When would the slaves be sold? _____

_____

2. Where would the sale take place? _____

_____

3. Why is the owner selling them? _____

_____

4. What are some of the skills these slaves have? _____

_____

5. Why are there no last names given? _____

_____

6. Does the owner show respect for the slaves as human beings? _____

_____

Explain your answer. _____

_____

The Owner of the following named and valuable Slaves, being on the eve of departure for Europe, will cause the same to be offered for sale, at the NEW EXCHANGE, corner of St. Louis and Chartres Streets, on Saturday, May 16, at Twelve o'Clock, *viz*.

1. SARAH, a mulattress, aged 45 years, a good cook and accustomed to housework in general, is an excellent and faithful nurse for sick persons and in every respect a first-rate character.

2. DENNIS, her son, a mulatto, aged 24 years, a first-rate cook and steward for a vessel, having been in that capacity for many years on board one of the Mobile packers; is strictly honest, temperate, and a first-rate subject.

3. CHLOE, a mulattress, aged 36 years, is, without exception, one of the most competent servants in the country, a first-rate washer and ironer, does up lace, a good cook, and for a bachelor who wishes a housekeeper, she would be invaluable; she is also a good ladies' maid, having traveled to the North in that capacity.

4. FANNY, her daughter, a mulattress, aged 16 years, speaks French and English, is a superior hairdresser, a good seamstress and ladies' maid, is smart, intelligent, and a first-rate character.

5. DANDRIDGE, a mulatto, aged 26 years, a first-rate dining room servant, a good painter and carpenter, and has but few equals for honesty and sobriety.

6. NANCY, his wife, aged about 24 years, a confidential house servant, good seamstress, cook, washer, ironer, etc.

7. MARY ANN, her child, a creole, aged 7 years, speaks French and English, is smart, active, and intelligent.

8. FANNY OR FRANCES, a mulattress, aged 22 years, is a first-rate washer and ironer, good cook and house servant, and has an excellent character.

9. EMMA, an orphan, aged 10 or 11 years, speaks French and English, has been in slavery seven years, has been accustomed to waiting on table, sewing, etc., is intelligent and active.

10. FRANK, a mulatto, aged about 32 years, speaks French and English, is a first-rate hunter and marksman, understands perfectly well the management of horses, and is in every respect a first-rate character, with the exception that he will occasionally drink, though not an habitual drunkard.

New Orleans, May 13, 1835.

Name _____

Date _____

STUDYING A CARTOON

Cartoons appeared in newspapers before the American Revolution—and ever since. Cartoonists use a drawing to make a point, using as few words as possible.

Below is the most famous cartoon printed in Colonial times. It was printed in the Pennsylvania Gazette by Benjamin Franklin. Study it and then answer the following questions.

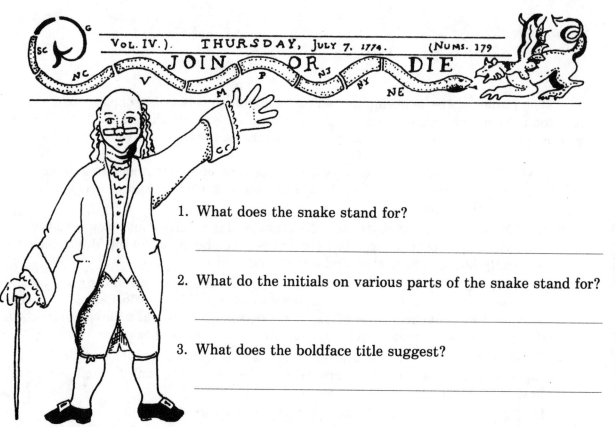

1. What does the snake stand for?

_____

2. What do the initials on various parts of the snake stand for?

_____

3. What does the boldface title suggest?

_____

4. The creature to the right is the mythical griffen—part eagle, part lion. It is a symbol used frequently on British flags. Why is it in this cartoon?

_____

_____

5. How often did the Gazette publish? How can you tell?

_____

_____

Name _____

Date _____

LET'S DISCUSS THIS

Everyday problems from real life situations can stimulate your reasoning ability. To discuss their solutions you will need to be able to analyze what you already know, reflect on your past learning, and synthesize knowledge from your social studies.

Read each of these problems and prepare yourself for discussing them in class by taking notes. Use the lines below and a separate sheet of paper to write your notes.

1. Many Americans are killed each year in traffic accidents. More than half of fatal accidents involve drivers who have been drinking alcoholic beverages just before driving. How can we reduce the number of fatal traffic accidents?

2. Jane has been writing to a pen pal in England. She just learned that her pen pal and her parents will be visiting Jane's city this summer. What plans should Jane make?

3. The City Council plans to move some recovering drug addicts into a run-down house on your block. They plan to fix the old house up before moving in the six recovering drug addicts. Your father is opposed to the city's buying the old house for such a purpose. Your mother thinks it's a good idea. How do you feel?

_____

_____

_____

_____

_____

_____

_____

_____

_____

_____

_____

_____

Name _____

Date _____

RECOGNIZING PROPAGANDA

One propaganda technique is name-calling. It is a way of putting a label on a person or product. Writers and speakers use these words to make a person or thing look good or bad. When reading or listening be on the alert for name-calling.

Pretend that you are in a courtroom. The district attorney is talking to the jury. In his summary to the jury he uses twelve "name-calling" words. See if you can pick them out from the summary below. Remember, some are used to make a person look better while most are used to make the accused look worse. Underline the twelve name-calling terms.

On Friday, March 3rd, a vicious gunman with drug-glazed eyes approached the teller's window with a poorly written note. The wording showed that the robber was desperate and dangerous.

The usually calm and efficient teller, Mrs. Mary Jones, a hard-working widow, did as she was told in the note. She placed stacks of fifty-dollar bills into his bag.

After a menacing gesture to the handicapped man on line behind him, the high-school–drop-out robber pushed his way out of the bank.

---

6 chapter

activities for SOLVING MATH PROBLEMS WITH UNDERSTANDING

The following activities provide your students with many experiences in applying thinking skills to math. By understanding what is expected and what is asked, your students have a better chance of getting things done. Answer keys for every activity can be found at the end of the book.

6-1 FIND THE MISSING NUMBER helps your students see how numbers relate to one another. One number has been removed in a sequence of five. The students must figure out the relationship among the given numbers in order to discover the missing number.

6-2 EXTRA DATA gives eight problems. In each one, more numbers than needed are included. Your students must come up with the correct answer. As an added activity, have your students circle the numbers not needed for the problem's solution.

6-3 SOLVING TIME PROBLEMS emphasizes estimation and time. Review the use of A.M. and P.M.

6-4 MAKE AN ESTIMATE helps your students estimate or approximate a realistic answer before they actually begin to compute. Be sure your students choose one of the three answers *before* they actually begin to compute. For more able students, you may want to cover up the three choices and have them write down their own estimate before they compute.

6-5 VISITING THE SEAPORT MUSEUM asks the students to solve six problems using a chart listing the number of visitors to a museum. When students finish, they are rewarded with three jokes loosely related to the activity.

6-6 EIGHT DIVIDED BY TWO IS . . . reviews important division skills.

6-7 SUCH LARGE NUMBERS! gives students practice in handling large numbers. Your students, presented with the popular vote in ten presidential elections, need to use the facts given to answer six questions. You can follow up by using the almanac to discuss results of any recent elections.

6-8 USING THE INFORMATION GIVEN presents a practical, school-life problem for students to solve. Based on prices for school-lunch snacks, this activity involves budgeting and computation.

6-9 WHAT FACTS DO I NEED? gives your students a chart of the caloric content of popular foods. They are asked to calculate total calories consumed based on different menus.

6–10 ESTIMATES VS. ACTUAL ANSWERS emphasizes students' skills in estimating.

6–11 WHICH OPERATION DO I USE? emphasizes the students' need to check the reasonableness of an answer before arriving at a solution.

6–12 THE SCIENCE OF STATISTICS assembles data into tabular form so your students can see the relationship between blocks of time. For enrichment, cover up two or three of the larger numbers before making copies of the page and ask students to compute them.

6–13 USE YOUR HEAD! gives five brainteasers that are to be solved *mentally*—without using pencil and paper. For slower students, you can cover the directions before making copies of the page and ask them to solve the problems with pencil and paper.

6–14 THE ANNUAL COUNTRY FAIR reviews important division skills.

6–15 UNNECESSARY FACTS asks your students to decide if too many or too few facts are given in order to solve seven problems. If enough data are given, your students are asked to solve the problem.

6–16 A FRACTION OF A PROBLEM offers ten fraction problems. Review fractional parts before having the students do this activity.

6–17 WHICH RULE APPLIES ? summarizes three rules of division by 2, 4, and 8. There are 12 exercises here for students to check their understanding of the rules.

6–18 SOLVING MONEY PROBLEMS is a nonalgebraic approach to coin problems. For example, in question 1, have your students multiply 8 by 25. Then, subtract $2.00 from $4.20, leaving $2.20. This will yield 22 dimes.

6–19 A + B = C is an exercise for your more able math students. They are asked to change each letter to a number. The example BY ÷ C = A can be any number of solutions: $12 \div 4 = 3$, $21 \div 7 = 3$, $42 \div 7 = 6$, and so on.

Name _____

Date _____

FIND THE MISSING NUMBER

Let's look at this sequence of five numbers:

3   7   11   _____   19

First, you notice that one number is missing. If you are asked to find the missing number, you must first see how the other numbers relate to one another. For one thing, they get larger. How much larger? They increase in size by four. $3 + 4 = 7$ $7 + 4 = 11$
We can assume the missing number is 15 because $11 + 4 = 15$ *and* $15 + 4 = 19$.

Try these. In some of the problems the numbers get smaller.

a.   9   11   _____   15   17

b.   4   _____   12   16   20

c.   2   7   12   _____   22

d.   0   _____   12   18   24

e.   43   38   _____   28   23

f.   7   14   21   28   _____

g.   120   98   _____   64   42

h.   0   _____   36   54   72

i.   3   _____   17   24   31

j.   51   74   97   _____   143

Name _____

Date _____

EXTRA DATA

Some word problems contain more numbers than you need to solve them. In each of these problems read what is asked for and then find solutions. Use only the information you need. Check your answer to be sure it makes sense.

1. Tony's new camera uses 35mm film. He shot a 12-exposure roll and a 24-exposure roll on his trip. Three pictures did not come out. How many pictures did come out?

   _____

2. On Tony's tour bus were 43 people. His album shows pictures of 29 adults and 6 children, including Tony. How many people do not appear in Tony's album?

   _____

3. Tony's class has 32 pupils. His teacher took a picture showing 4 rows of 8 pupils each. How many pupils are in the class picture?

   _____

4. Tony bought a photo album that contains 12 pages. He put 8 pictures on each page. He has filled 9 pages. How many pictures are in his album?

   _____

5. Mr. Esposito has three children at Bryant School. The school picture package costs $9.50 per child. How much will it cost Mr. Esposito to buy three packages of pictures?

   _____

6. Tony bought two rolls of film that cost $2.39 each, including 5 percent tax. How much change would he get from a five-dollar bill?

   _____

7. A roll of 24 exposures costs $3.75. A roll of 36 exposures costs $4.45. How much would Mr. Esposito spend if he bought two rolls of each?

   _____

8. Mr. Esposito pays 25 cents for each print at the drugstore. He pays 19 cents for each print when he mails his film away. How much will it cost for 24 prints at the drugstore?

   _____

Name _____

Date _____

SOLVING TIME PROBLEMS

In solving these time problems you will have to be aware of time of day. Remember A.M. is used with times from midnight to noon, and P.M. is used with times from noon to midnight. Label your answer to each problem with A.M. or P.M.

1. The trip to Philadelphia takes 4 hours and 15 minutes. If the Keyes family leaves at 11 A.M., at what time will they arrive?

_____

2. A bus tour of Philadelphia leaves at 9:15 A.M. It lasts 2 hours and 30 minutes. At what time is it over?

_____

3. It takes 20 minutes for the Lawn Kare man to mow each lawn on Elm Street. If there are 9 lawns for him to mow, when will he finish if he begins at 9:00 A.M.?

_____

4. Marie's plane was to land at 2:15 P.M. It was 40 minutes late, due to a storm. At what time did it arrive?

_____

5. Mrs. Riccardi took John to the zoo. They arrived at 11:10 A.M. and left 1 hour and 30 minutes later. At what time did they leave?

_____

6. Mr. Klein arrived home at 7:10 P.M. If his trip took 1 hour and 15 minutes, at what time did he leave work?

_____

7. The actors must be at the theater 90 minutes before curtain time. If curtain time is 8:40 P.M., at what time must the actors be at the theater?

_____

8. Mr. Felix left the doctor's office at 8:15 P.M. He had been there for 2 hours and 30 minutes. At what time did he arrive?

Name _____

Date _____

MAKE AN ESTIMATE

The solution to many verbal math problems can be checked if you *estimate* your answers before you begin to solve the problems. By estimating first, silly or outrageous answers can be eliminated. Underline your estimate to each of these problems.

COOKIE SALES AT THE TYLER SCHOOL

1. The Student Council sells packages of cookies for 25 cents each. The Council sold $40 worth one day. This was about how many packages?   50   150   500

2. The cookies cost 18 cents. If they sell 100 packages of cookies at 25 cents, about how much do the pupils earn?   75¢ $7.50 $75

3. Of the 100 packages of cookies sold on Wednesday, 50 were chocolate chip, 17 were peanut butter, 9 were vanilla, and the rest were coconut. About how many were coconut?   5   20   25

4. If the students earn 84 cents on each dozen sold and they sold 12 dozen one week, about how much did they earn? $8 $10 $12

5. On Monday, 24 packages were sold; Tuesday, 30 packages; Wednesday, 42 packages; Thursday, 18 packages; and Friday, 36 packages. Were the average sales per day about 18, 28, or 38 packages?

6. A teacher wants to buy one 25-cent package for each child in her class. There are 32 pupils. About how much will this cost? $5 $9 $12

7. Each tray holds 12 packages. Each carton holds 15 trays. Will a carton hold about 75, 175, or 225 packages?

8. If there are 3 cookies in a package and the teacher bought 32 packages, about how many individual cookies did she buy?   75   100   144

9. When counting the coins for the bank, the treasurer rolled 40 quarters and 50 dimes. Was this about $10, $15, or $25?

10. On a busy day the students took in $42.25. About how many 25-cent packages of cookies were sold that day?   70   170   270

Name _____

Date _____

VISITING THE SEAPORT MUSEUM

Use the following chart to solve the problems below it:

VISITORS TO THE SEAPORT MUSEUM

Time	Mon.	Tues.	Wed.	Thurs.	Fri.
9–12	134	165	152	137	196
12–5	379	347	369	365	347

1. How many visitors came to the Museum on these days?

   Monday _____   Wednesday _____   Friday _____

2. Were there more visitors on Tuesday or Thursday? How many more? _____

   _____

3. Estimate the number of visitors on Monday and Tuesday of the week on the chart.

   _____

4. Estimate the total number of afternoon visitors that week. _____

5. How many more visitors came in the afternoon of each day? _____

6. What was the average morning attendance? _____

HUMOROUS HIGHLIGHTS

Now that you have finished your problem solving, here are three jokes relating to the sea and seasickness:

There's no place like Venice.
Where else can you get seasick crossing the street?

"I always get seasick the first day out."
"Then why don't you go a day late?"

"Shall I bring your dinner on the deck, sir?"
"No, just throw it overboard and save time."

Name _____

Date _____

EIGHT DIVIDED BY TWO IS . . .

Practice your thinking skills and division number facts by answering these questions.

1. List 10 numbers between 100 and 999 that are divisible by 4.

    _____

2. How many multiples of 8 are there between 205 and 250? List them.

    _____

3. I bought a box of 36 cookies. Some were eaten. When I count the cookies that are left by 4's, I have 2 left over. When I count them by 5's I have 1 left over. How many cookies are left in the box?

    _____

4. Which costs less: 15 ounces of juice for $1.35 or 24 ounces of juice for $1.92?

    _____

5. Make up a 6-digit number that is evenly divisible by 2, 4, and 8, and does NOT end in 0.

    _____

6. How many miles does Mr. Smith's car get per gallon of gasoline if he drove 112 miles on 8 gallons?

    _____

7. If Jamie earned $25.40 for 4 hours' work, how much did she earn per hour?

    $ _____

8. Mr. Bauer needs 118 vinyl tiles to cover a floor. If the tiles come 12 to a package, how many packages should he buy?

    _____

Name _____

Date _____

SUCH LARGE NUMBERS!

The following table shows the popular vote for the winners and losers for ten presidential elections. Use the facts you need to answer the questions below.

Year	President Elected	Popular Vote	Losing Candidate	Popular Vote
1824	John Quincy Adams	105,321	Andrew Jackson	155,872
			Henry Clay	46,587
			William Crawford	44,282
1828	Andrew Jackson	647, 231	John Quincy Adams	509,097
1832	Andrew Jackson	687,502	Henry Clay	530,189
1836	Martin Van Buren	762,678	William H. Harrison	548,007
1840	William H. Harrison	1,275,017	Martin Van Buren	1,128,702
1844	James A. Polk	1,337,243	Henry Clay	1,299,068
1848	Zachary Taylor	1,360,101	Lewis Cass	1,220,544
1852	Franklin Pierce	1,601,474	Winfield Scott	1,386,578
1856	James C. Buchanan	1,927,995	John C. Fremont	1,391,555
1860	Abraham Lincoln	1,866,352	Stephen A. Douglas	1,375,157
			John C. Breckinridge	845,763
			John Bell	589,581

1. How many votes were cast altogether in 1824? _____

2. How many more votes did Andrew Jackson get in 1832 than in 1828? _____

3. What was unusual about the elections of 1836 and 1840? _____

_____

4. How many people voted in 1860 for candidates that lost the election? _____

5. Did more people vote in 1856 or in 1852? _____

6. How many more votes did Henry Clay receive the second time he ran? _____

Name _____

Date _____

USING THE INFORMATION GIVEN

Gloria Gomez gets $3 each week from her mother with which to buy a snack in school. This is in addition to her school lunch money. The prices of each snack are:

Brownies 30¢ (one)
Fruit drink 35¢ (can)
Chocolate chip cookies 25¢ (package of three)
Ice-cream 40¢ (bar or cup)

Using the information given, solve each of these problems;

1. If Gloria buys a package of cookies and a can of fruit drink each day of a five-day

   week will she have any money left over? _____ Will $3 be enough

   to buy both items each day? _____

2. Gloria had an ice-cream bar on Monday, Wednesday, and Friday. On Tuesday and

   Thursday she bought a brownie. How much did she spend? _____

3. If Gloria had a brownie the first four days of the week, how much money did she

   have left to spend on Friday? _____

4. Gloria saves 35 cents of her snack money each week. How much is there left for Gloria
   to spend each day assuming she plans to spend the same amount each of the five

   days? _____

5. One week, Gloria spent all of her money on cookies. How many individual cookies

   did she buy? (**Hint:** Each 25-cent package contains three individual cookies.) _____

Name _____

Date _____

WHAT FACTS DO I NEED?

This table shows the number of calories* found in some common foods. Use these facts to solve the problems.

CALORIE CHART

Hamburger, regular	245	Milk, glass	165
Hamburger, lean	152	Cheese, cheddar, slice	110
Ham, lean slice	195	Egg, large	90
Chicken, 2 slices, roasted	230	Potato, baked	90
Bread, white, slice	55	Apple, medium	75

1. Juan has a lunch made up of two slices of roast chicken, two slices of bread, a slice of cheddar cheese, and a *half* glass of milk. How many calories was that?

   _____

2. Mrs. Johnson is on a diet. She chose a lean hamburger instead of a regular burger and an apple instead of a baked potato. How many calories did she save?

   _____

3. Mr. Colon wants to eat no more than 3,000 calories a day. Lunch is a sandwich made up of two slices of bread, two lean slices of ham, one slice of cheddar cheese, and a cup of black coffee (no calories). How many calories can he eat at his two other meals?

   _____

4. Using the chart, plan two different lunches. You may want to include some calorie-free diet soda or a cup of ice cream, which has 310 calories. Plan one lunch for under 800 calories and one for under 1,400 calories. Write your menus on the back of this sheet.

*We use the term "calorie" to mean a measure of energy made by food once it's eaten. So, a glass of milk has the potential to give you more energy than a slice of bread. Calories *not* used as energy are stored in the body as fat.

Name _____

Date _____

ESTIMATES VS. ACTUAL ANSWERS

Sidney collects bottle caps. He feels they will increase in value in the future. He now has a collection of 536 caps.

Solve these problems based on Sidney's collection. Estimate your answer before solving each problem.

1. At four caps for a penny, how much is Sidney's collection worth?

   (Estimate: _____)   (Actual answer: _____)

2. If he could get a dime for every sixteen caps, how much would he earn?

   (Estimate: _____)   (Actual answer: _____)

3. If he sold one fourth of his collection for half a penny per cap, how much money would he get?

   (Estimate: _____)   (Actual answer: _____)

4. Sidney was able to store 90 caps in a shoe box. How many boxes would he need to store all of his caps?

   (Estimate: _____)   (Actual answer: _____)

5. If one eighth of his collection came from cola bottles and half of the remaining caps were from root beer, how many came from root beer?

   (Estimate: _____)   (Actual answer: _____)

6. Eventually Sidney's collection filled nine and one half shoe boxes. How many caps did that represent?

   (Review question 4)   (Estimate: _____)   (Actual Answer: _____)

Name _____

Date _____

WHICH OPERATION DO I USE?

You know how to multiply, divide, add, and subtract. For each of these problems apply the appropriate operation and check your work. Make sure your answer makes sense.

1. Jimmy has part of a sheet of stamps. They are twenty-cent stamps. There are 4 rows with 8 stamps in each row.

   a. How many stamps in all? _____

   b. How much are these stamps worth? _____

2. In Room 112 there are 3 rows of seats with 7 pupils in each row. There are also 2 tables with 5 pupils at each table. What is the total number of pupils? _____

3. Carol bought a 69-cent pen. She gave the clerk 3 quarters. How much change will she get? _____

4. It takes the Kim family 6 hours to drive to the mountains. If they arrive at 4 P.M. at what time did they start out? _____

5. One brand of tuna fish costs 98 cents a can. Another brand sells for $1.19. If you were to buy 3 cans, how much would you save by buying the cheaper brand? _____

Name _____

Date _____

THE SCIENCE OF STATISTICS

Statistics is the science of collecting and classifying facts. We have collected various blocks of time: months, weeks, days, and hours. Your job is to arrange these blocks of time in order. Start with the smallest (12 months) and place it in box #1.

DATA

12 months	105 weeks	2,000 days	50,000 hours
30 months	160 weeks	1,500 days	35,000 hours
51 months	250 weeks	750 days	10,000 hours
26 months	60 weeks	3,000 days	30,000 hours
55 months	350 weeks	400 days	20,000 hours

1.	2.	3.	4.
5.	6.	7.	8.
9.	10.	11.	12.
13.	14.	15.	16.
17.	18.	19.	20.

Name _____

Date _____

USE YOUR HEAD!

These brain-teasers can be solved *without* using paper or pencil. Use your pencil to circle the answer *only*.

1. Which of these is the best way to estimate the answer for the example: 3.16×5.83?

   a. 4×6 c. 4×5

   b. 3×6 d. 3×5

2. Which of these is the smallest number?

   a. 1.15   c. 1.5

   b. 1.05   d. 1.10

3. Which of these decimals is closest in value to .5?

   a. .399   c. .412

   b. .602   d. .634

4. Which of these numbers is .03 less than 6.547?

   a. 6.247   c. 6.517

   b. 3.547   d. 6.544

5. Which of these fractions is closest in value to 65 percent?

   a. 3/5   c. 2/3

   b. 3/4   d. 5/8

Name _____

Date _____

THE ANNUAL COUNTRY FAIR

Many everyday verbal problems are solved using the process of division. When there are remainders you have to put on your "thinking cap" when coming up with your answer. Use division to solve these problems.

1. Mrs. Kay has 150 prizes to give out. There are 12 booths at the fair. How many prizes should she leave at each booth? There will be an additional prize at 6 booths. Why?

   _____

2. Mr. Lee said he would blow up the balloons to decorate each of the 12 booths. He blew up 106 balloons.
   How many balloons did each booth receive? _____

   How many booths got 1 extra balloon? _____

3. Ms. Dee volunteered to make jelly apples. She made 147 and sold out in 3 hours.

   How many did she sell per hour? _____

4. The 8 members of the service squad bought $100 worth of tickets.

   How many tickets' worth did they each buy or average? _____

5. There are 100 ride tickets per roll. The Whip costs 6 tickets per ride. The Wheel

   costs 8 tickets per ride. One roll will provide how many Whip tickets? _____

   How many Wheel tickets? _____

6. If a roll of 100 ride tickets cost $10, how much does a Whip ride cost in dollars and

   cents? _____

7. How much less does a Whip ticket cost than a Wheel ticket in cents? _____

8. How many children can ride the Whip if 4 rolls are purchased? _____

Name _____

Date _____

UNNECESSARY FACTS

Some problems contain facts not useful for the solution. Solve these problems using only the needed facts. A few problems will have a necessary fact missing. In that case, write in what is missing as your answer.

1. A farmer planted 34 corn plants in a row and 24 tomato plants in a row. If he planted 75 rows of corn, how many corn plants were set out to grow?

   _____

2. The same farmer set out 26 rows of tomato plants. He hoped to get an average of 30 tomatoes per plant. About how many tomatoes will he harvest?

   _____

3. He also planted potatoes. He picked 17 bushels of large potatoes and 14 bushels of small ones. The store paid him $16 a bushel for the large potatoes. How much did he earn for the small ones?

   _____

4. The farmer's daughter grew 120 strawberry plants. She sold them for $2.50 a basket at a roadside stand. How much money did she earn?

   _____

5. The farmer was taxed $3,720 each year on his land. In addition, he paid a water tax of $724. If he paid his land tax in 12 equal monthly installments, how much was each payment?

   _____

6. If he paid both the land and water tax together in monthly installments, what would be each month's total tax bill?

   _____

7. The county gave a 3 percent discount to farmers who paid their water tax in advance. How much could this farmer save a year by paying in advance?

   _____

6–16

Name ______________________

Date ______________________

A FRACTION OF A PROBLEM

You may want to use some scrap paper to solve these problems.

1. John and José made 14 paper airplanes. If José made $\frac{1}{2}$ of these planes, how many did he make?

   ____

2. Which of these fractions is larger than $\frac{1}{2}$? ____________

   $\frac{1}{2}$ $\frac{1}{4}$ $\frac{1}{6}$ $\frac{1}{8}$

3. Don finished his homework in 30 minutes. Jane completed the same assignment in

   $\frac{1}{2}$ that time. How long did it take her to finish? ____________

4. What fractional part of an hour did Don use to finish? ____________

   Jane? ____________

5. Which fraction tells us that there is 1 chance in 3 that it will rain tomorrow? ______

   $\frac{2}{3}$ $\frac{1}{2}$ $\frac{1}{3}$ $\frac{3}{1}$

6. What fraction is another name for 0.5? ____________

7. Which fraction is equal to "three fourths"? ____________

   $\frac{2}{3}$ $\frac{4}{5}$ $\frac{6}{8}$ $\frac{8}{10}$

8. Which fraction names the greatest number? ____________

   $\frac{5}{12}$ $\frac{1}{3}$ $\frac{2}{4}$ $\frac{5}{6}$

9. Arrange these fractions in order of size. List the *smallest* fraction first.

   $\frac{2}{5}$ $\frac{3}{7}$ $\frac{4}{5}$ $\frac{3}{8}$ $\frac{4}{9}$

   ____

10. Arrange the fractions in order of size. List the *largest* fraction first.

    $\frac{5}{9}$ $\frac{7}{8}$ $\frac{3}{4}$ $\frac{5}{8}$ $\frac{5}{6}$

    ____

Name _____

Date _____

WHICH RULE APPLIES?

By now, you certainly know if a number can be divided by 5. It ends with a 5 or 0. Study these three rules:

1. A number is divisible by 2 if it ends in an even number. (Examples: 4, 10, 22, 104)
2. A number is divisible by 4 if the last *two* digits are a multiple of 4 or they are both zeros, as in 216 or 200. (Examples: 16, 124, 208, 336)
3. A number is divisible by 8 if the last *three* digits are a multiple of 8 or if they are all zeros, as in 1,424 or 3,000. (Examples: 168, 264, 472, 648)

Check your understanding of these rules by studying each number below. Alongside the number put a 2, 4, or 8 when that number goes into the larger number evenly. For some, you will have two or three answers.

a. 1,505 _____   g. 7,024 _____

b. 2,556 _____   h. 4,916 _____

c. 6,848 _____   i. 9,624 _____

d. 5,472 _____   j. 5,344 _____

e. 3,241 _____   k. 1,476 _____

f. 6,001 _____   l. 9,444 _____

Name _____

Date _____

SOLVING MONEY PROBLEMS

You may want to use trial and error to solve these problems. After some practice you may want to make a chart to help solve these coin problems.

1. Jerry has a jar with 8 quarters and many more dimes. Altogether he has $4.20 in his collection of these two coins. How many dimes does Jerry have?

   _____

2. His sister Jean has 12 quarters and lots of dimes. She has $10 in all. How many dimes does Jean have?

   _____

3. Felix has a collection of dimes and quarters that equal $5. He has six more quarters than he has dimes. How many of each coin does Felix have?

   _____

4. Danny's collection of nickels and dimes totals $2.25. He has three times as many nickels as dimes. How many dimes has Danny?

   _____

5. Sheila has twice as many dimes as quarters. She has $4.50 all together. How many quarters does Sheila have?

   _____

6. Annette has an equal number of nickels and dimes. She has a total of $7.50 in the two coins. How many does she have of each coin?

   _____

Name _____

Date _____

A + B = C

Change each letter to a number, not necessarily its place in the alphabet. All the same letters must be changed to the same number. All different letters must be different numbers.

Example: BY ÷ C = A
$$12 \div 4 = 3$$

1. BA
    BA
    + BA
    ─────
    AJ

2. OF
    OF
    OF
    + OF
    ─────
    TO

3. HE
    + E
    ─────
    EH

4. P
    P
    + P
    ─────
    UP

Hints:

1. a. All three addends are the same.
   b. The units number in the addend is the same as the tens number in the sum.
   c. The sum is less than 100.
   d. Each addend is less than 33.

2. a. All four addends are the same.
   b. The tens number of each addend is the same as the units number of the sum.
   c. The sum is more than 100.
   d. Each addend is more than 25.

7 chapter

activities for
ORGANIZING INFORMATION FOR RETENTION

Very often a good lesson is just not enough because the students don't always retain what they learn. In order to remember what they know, students must first organize the information. The following activities help your students do just that. Answer keys for every activity can be found at the end of the book.

7-1 ON YOUR MARK . . . provides students with practice in seeing what qualities a given group of words have in common. You can expand upon this list by using words from the students' science and social studies textbooks.

7-2 THE SENSES helps your students become aware of the various senses that contribute to memory. Students must realize that they can learn with more than just their eyes.

7-3 IT'S ON THE HOUSE! gives your students practice in visualizing a list as a whole entity. You can help slower students by supplying the "whole" word. Your more able students might enjoy the humor at the bottom of the page. If you don't want to include the jokes, just cover them up before making copies of the sheet.

7-4 IMPORTANT FACTS helps students fix upon important items for recall by underlining key facts as they read a passage.

7-5 TIMES, PLACES, PEOPLE, OBJECTS also asks your students to underline key facts in sentences. For homework, you may want to have students bring in a newspaper article that they have underlined and put into list form.

7-6 PREPARING AN OUTLINE asks students to outline material they want to commit to memory. For less able students, you can fill in more of the blanks before you make copies of the activity.

7-7 LEARNING TO MEMORIZE gives your students practice in using mnemonics as cues to memorizing.

7-8 THE BEGINNING, MIDDLE, AND END asks your students to become familiar with certain words that serve as "red flags." These order words help students put isolated sentences in sequential order. A good follow-up exercise is to have your students bring in a page from a magazine with these order words underlined.

7-9 B-E-A-M can stimulate more able students to construct their own lists of mnemonics. For less able students, you can start the mnemonic for them.

7-10 USING CONTEXT CLUES gives students practice in making use of the first or topic sentence of a paragraph. This, plus the use of context clues, will enable your students to practice the cloze technique. For slower students, you can fill in the first two blanks. For brighter students, you can cover up a few more key words before making copies of the sheet.

7-11 THE LONGEST RIVER helps your students handle bits of information in a meaningful way. The eight questions that follow the table of facts strengthen your students' abilities to organize and retain information. Supplemental activities might include organizing the rivers by length and listing the rivers by source location.

7-12 LINE FOR LINE! helps your students get information by carefully following very detailed instructions.

Name _____

Date _____

ON YOUR MARK . . .

Below you will find ten groups of words. Read each set or group to see what they have in common. Then, when you are sure what category most of the words belong to, cross out the word or name in each set that does *not* belong to that category. You may need to use a dictionary to look up some new words.

| **Example:** | red | blue | ~~bread~~ | green |

1. collie, beagle, beaver, poodle
2. python, cobra, rattler, snail
3. Iowa, Ohio, Maine, Atlanta
4. Oregon, California, Washington, Connecticut
5. heavy, large, big, immense
6. coal, stove, wood, oil
7. ax, drill, saw, chisel
8. liver, kidney, hip, brain
9. rice, corn, pecan, oats
10. puppy, hen, kitten, cub

Name _____

Date _____

THE SENSES

Look at this list of items. At one time in the past you experienced all or most of these things. To help you recall or remember these items you would use one of your senses. If you can tell what it is or was through your vision, put a "V" in front of the item. If it was mostly another sense, put "H" for hearing, "S" for smell, "T" for taste, or "F" for feel. You may want to list more than one sense.

_____ dog barking	_____ stiff collar	_____ electric shock
_____ wet socks	_____ bell ringing	_____ tomato juice
_____ bacon frying	_____ rough log	_____ mashed potatoes
_____ an empty bag	_____ open can of paint	_____ lightning
_____ sunbeam	_____ mumble	_____ baby powder
_____ onion flavor	_____ bumblebee	_____ modeling clay
_____ thunder	_____ screech of brakes	_____ snowball
_____ cards being shuffled	_____ white lie	_____ magic trick
_____ fingerpaint	_____ permed hair	_____ whipped cream
_____ peach pit	_____ sermon	_____ cough

© 1986 by Parker Publishing Company, Inc.

Name _____

Date _____

IT'S ON THE HOUSE!

You can remember things better if you can see or visualize them as a whole rather than trying to recall them as unrelated items. If you were asked to memorize this list—floor, walls, window, roof, cellar—you would find it easier to see the items as the parts of a *house*.

Use the visualizing technique to memorize the following lists of words. Make it easier for yourself by visualizing the whole for each list. You may have to stretch your imagination for some lists.

1. flour, butter, salt, water, sugar
2. wood, nails, screws, paint
3. page, cover, print, binding, title
4. chalk, chair, desk, flag, board
5. lettuce, onion, tomato, carrot, cucumber
6. chicken, rice, pepper, salt, broth
7. tire, fender, window, wheel, bumper
8. chain, wheel, handlebar, seat, pedal
9. dial, screen, tube, antenna, plug
10. sink, stove, refrigerator, dishwasher, cabinet

JOKES ON THE HOUSE

"Madam, this book will cut your housework in half."
"Good. I'll take two of them."

"Do these stairs take you to the second floor?"
"No, you'll have to walk."

"When will you straighten out the house, dear?"
"Why? Is it tilted?"

Name _____

Date _____

IMPORTANT FACTS

Read this passage about Florida. Locate or identify the important facts. Underline the words, numbers, or phrases that describe *times, places,* or *people.* Write them in the correct column. We have started each list for you.

Florida, at the southern tip of the East Coast, is a land of citrus fruits and resort cities. Many beaches stretch along its coast. Ponce de León discovered Florida in 1513 and claimed it for Spain. He named the land Florida because he saw so many flowers.

Because there are so many sunny days each year Florida is called the Sunshine State. It juts out into the sea for 400 miles. Key West, Florida, lies further south than any mainland city in the United States. St. Augustine, founded in 1565, is the country's oldest city. Tallahassee is the state capitol.

TIMES	PLACES	PEOPLE
1513	Florida	Ponce de León

Name _____

Date _____

TIMES, PLACES, PEOPLE, OBJECTS

In order to remember the important things or essential data about what you read, you need to classify them. You already know how to look for the "who," "what," "when," and "why." Now train yourself to underline the essential data in these sentences by looking for *times, places, people,* and *objects.* None of the sentences will have all four. After underlining, list the data below.

Example: On *Thursday, Joan* put her *car* in the *garage.*

---

1. Abraham Lincoln was born in Kentucky in 1809.
2. Henry Ford built one of the earliest automobiles.
3. Eleanor Roosevelt represented the United States in the United Nations.
4. Lake Mead in Nevada is 115 miles long and is one of the world's largest artificial lakes.
5. One member of the pine family that loses its needles every fall is the larch.
6. Leicester, England, is pronounced Lester and is known for its shoe factories and stocking mills.
7. Most of our lettuce comes from California and is planted in July.
8. John A. Logan was a Civil War general who in 1868 started the idea of Memorial Day.

TIMES	PLACES	PEOPLE	OBJECTS
Thursday	*garage*	*Joan*	*car*

Name _____

Date _____

PREPARING AN OUTLINE

An outline helps you organize ideas. It helps you put important facts in order. Roman numerals list the main topic. Capital letters list subtopics. Arabic numbers list details.

Use the topics and details in the box to fill in the outline. Three items have been done for you.

FIELD DAY

I. Committees

    A. _____

    B. _____

    C. *Food* _____

    D. _____

II. _____

    A. _____

        1. *Baseball diamond* _____

        2. _____

        3. _____

        4. _____

        5. _____

    B. _____

        1. _____

        2. *Kite-flying contest* _____

        3. _____

Main Topics
Activities
Committees

Subtopics
Food
Buses
Program
Special events
Athletic facilities
Guests

Details
Kite-flying contest
Baseball diamond
Tennis courts
Swimming pool
Outdoor track
Three-legged race
Soccer field
Tug-of-war

Name _____

Date _____

LEARNING TO MEMORIZE

Practice makes perfect! The more you practice developing a good memory the sooner you will have one. Study each group of words below using the study techniques you have learned—one line at a time. Use a piece of paper to cover the lines you are not up to yet. After you study one line of items, turn this paper over and see how many items you can recall. Write them down on the back of this paper. Learn one line perfectly before you go on to the next.

1. Foods found in America by the Colonists:

   tomatoes   chili   corn   potatoes   beans

2. Famous cities of Europe:

   Rome   Frankfurt   Paris   Lisbon   Oslo

3. City street scene:

   bus stop   newsstand   police station   traffic light   street lamp

4. Appliances found inside a house:

   TV   stove   hair dryer   radio   refrigerator

5. Items photographed on a trip to Africa:

   diamond mine   zebra   jungle   elephant   desert

Name _____

Date _____

THE BEGINNING, MIDDLE, AND END

Some sentences begin with "order words." These words help you put the sentences in sequence or order. Read each order word or words in this list. Decide whether you think the word(s) would most likely come near the *beginning*, near the *middle*, or near the *end* of a paragraph. Some of the order words can be used in two or three parts of a paragraph. Write "B," "M," or "E" alongside each order word, for *beginning, middle,* or *end.* Some order words will have two or more letters.

In conclusion _____*E*_____   So _____

First _____   For example _____

Next _____   Then _____

After that _____   When _____

Also _____   Third _____

Begin by _____   At last _____

Second _____   Later _____

Next _____   Lastly _____

Name _____

Date _____

B-E-A-M

Mnemonics is pronounced (knee-MON-iks). It means "aids to the memory" and comes from a Greek word. One popular type of mnemonic is to use the first letter of each item you want to remember to form a new word. For example, your mother asks you to get the following items at the store: *eggs, milk, bread, applesauce.* You might rearrange them, using the first letter of each item to spell:

BEAM (bread, eggs, applesauce, milk)

Use a similar mnemonic for each of these short lists. Then, write your mnemonic in the blank.

1. grapes, olives, lemons, dates _____

2. sugar, pepper, tissue, apples, eggs _____

3. Harry, Ronnie, Ida, Carl, Alex _____

4. clock, lamp, ruler, watch, apple _____

5. Jones, Klein, Collins, Anderson _____

6. paint, ruler, dropcloth, oil, paper, easel, remover _____

7. ribbon, carbon, paper, ink, eraser _____

Name _____

Date _____

USING CONTEXT CLUES

We can read the first sentence or title of a story to get clues as to what the paragraph or story is about. In the paragraph that follows *the first sentence will set the scene for you.* Then, read each sentence that has a missing word or words very carefully. Using context clues, put in a word in each space that will give sense to the paragraph as a whole.

    By the year 2084 many families will probably live on the moon. Life on the ____(1)____ will be very ____(2)____ from life as we know it on Earth. For example, a ten-year-old girl called Doreen will awaken at 7:00 ____(3)____ moontime. She puts on ____(4)____ special moonsuit ____(5)____, moonshoes, and then goes to ____(6)____ community bathroom. You see, everyone ____(7)____ the ____(8)____ lives together in ____(9)____ large bubble-shaped house. Doreen must ____(10)____ the heavy moonshoes because the ____(11)____ of gravity is different. The shoes' weight helps ____(12)____ her from floating in air. Because the gases of the atmosphere are different she must ____(13)____ a plastic dome over her ____(14)____. Sometimes she wishes she were ____(15)____ on Earth.

(1) _____   (6) _____   (11) _____

(2) _____   (7) _____   (12) _____

(3) _____   (8) _____   (13) _____

(4) _____   (9) _____   (14) _____

(5) _____   (10) _____   (15) _____

Name _____

Date _____

THE LONGEST RIVER

This is an alphabetical list of rivers in the United States that are 350 or more miles long and the location of their source. After you have studied the list, answer the questions below.

RIVER	LENGTH	SOURCE LOCATION
Alabama	735 miles	Alabama
Arkansas	1,459	Colorado
Cimarron	600	New Mexico
Colorado	1,450	Colorado
Columbia	1,243	Canada
Green	730	Wyoming
Mississippi	2,348	Minnesota
Missouri	2,315	Montana
Ohio	981	Pennsylvania
Ohio-Allegheny	1,306	Pennsylvania
Red	1,270	Oklahoma
Rio Grande	1,885	Colorado
Snake	1,038	Wyoming
Wabash	529	Ohio
White	720	Arkansas
Yellowstone	674	Wyoming
Yukon	1,770	Canada

1. List the seventeen rivers in order of size. Start with the shortest. Which one is in the middle of your list? _____

2. How much longer is the Mississippi River than the Wabash? _____

3. Three rivers on our list have their source in Wyoming. Which rivers are they?

_____   _____   _____

4. Which is the longer of the two rivers that have their source in Canada?

_____

5. Two rivers have similar names. One is 325 miles longer than the other. Which is the longer river of the two? _____

6. Of the Red, Green, and White Rivers, which two are almost the same length?

_____   _____

7. Which river is closest to the Cimarron in length? _____

8. Which is the third longest river on the list? _____

Name _____

Date _____

LINE FOR LINE!

Read the instructions in the problems below carefully. Carry them out on these three lines.

#1	57	64	37	25	98
#2	P	T	R	S	O	U	V
#3	man	coat	hug	jump

1. On line 1 circle the number that is one more than (6 × 6) and on line 3 circle the second and third letters of the third word.

2. Circle the middle letter on line 2, the first letter of the fourth word on line 3, and the number equal to (5 × 5).

3. Put a cross on the letter before S on line 2, a cross on the "o" in line 3, a square around the number equal to (10 × 10) minus 2, and a circle around the second vowel in the second word on line 3.

4. Put a square around the last consonant in the last word on line 3 and a cross on the smaller of the two remaining numbers untouched on line 1.

5. Put a circle around the letter after U and a line through the "um" in the last word on line 3.

6. Put a cross on the letter before T on line 2; put a circle around the first word in line 3 and a cross on the last letter of the second word; put a cross on the number equal to (8 × 8).

7. Look at the remaining letters that have not been touched by a circle, a line, or a cross. What word do they spell?

8 chapter

activities for INTERPRETING SCIENTIFIC DATA

Every day, the world is introduced to more and more scientific facts and data. Helping children learn how to use these data, interpret these facts, and think through life situations in a scientific manner is the main idea behind the following activities. Answer keys for every activity can be found at the end of the book.

8-1 **WHICH CITY?** introduces students to a list of data from which they have to extract factual answers. Some simple math procedures are required. For less able students, ask them to list the cities in order of inches of rain that fell. For brighter students, ask for the average (or the mean and median) rainfalls of the cities listed.

8-2 **WHERE DO I FIND SEAWEED?** can be adapted for older students by making more sophisticated lists, such as items found in a hardware store or in a physics lab or in a photo darkroom.

8-3 **COMPARING MATTER** gives three answers to help get your students started. For brighter students, you can cover up the three answers before making copies of the sheet.

8-4 **THREE KINDS OF ENERGY** can be simplified for slower students by asking them to set up a table of two columns: chemical energy and mechanical energy. By eliminating the material on electrical energy, the students will avoid feelings of frustration. More able students can be asked to expand the list from eight items to fifteen.

8-5 **HOW MUCH OXYGEN?** gives students a chance to work alone or in a small group, in which they can record the breaths per minute of partners.

8-6 **PHYSICAL VS. CHEMICAL PROPERTIES** describes physical and chemical properties in detail and asks students to identify ten descriptions of phenomena.

8-7 **YOUR POWERS OF OBSERVATION I** helps students practice their ability to recall what they have seen. Questions 4 through 6 provoke some serious thought on the part of your students.

8-8 **CONDUCTION VS. CONVECTION** is similar in format to activity 8-6. Students are asked to distinguish between conduction and convection.

8-9 THINKING ABOUT BUOYANCY asks students to experiment with buoyancy as they float their own boats made from aluminum foil.

8-10 YOUR POWERS OF OBSERVATION II further tests students' skill in observation. For less able students, change the word "percentage" in question 5 to "number."

8-11 SEEING IS BELIEVING guides students in their observations. After completing the six questions, you can pose this enrichment question: "What caused the raisins to rise and sink?" Some students may need to use reference books to answer this question.

8-12 THE BERMUDA TRIANGLE MYSTERY asks your students to put on their thinking caps! They will recall previous learning. They will also need to use a globe.

8-13 LEARNING ABOUT SAMPLING offers a hands-on approach to help students understand probability. A portable typewriter or computer keyboard can be used. If these are not available, make copies of a paragraph (from a textbook or a magazine) already typed.

8-14 LET'S EXPERIMENT WITH CHARCOAL describes an easy-to-do experiment.

8-15 WHY DOES IT CHANGE? lends itself easily to small-group instruction because all students get to do something. Three or four students can work on each experiment.

Name _____

Date _____

WHICH CITY?

Here are ten American cities and the amounts of rain that fell there in inches in a recent year. Refer to this list when you answer the questions below.

Baltimore	41.62	Minneapolis	43.56
Boston	41.55	New York	41.18
Chicago	43.66	Philadelphia	42.15
Hartford	43.00	Portland	43.77
Louisville	42.94	San Francisco	43.62

1. Which city had the least rainfall?

_____

2. Which city had the most rainfall?

_____

3. Baltimore had exactly two inches less rain than what other city?

_____

4. Which city came closest to Louisville in the amount of rain that year?

_____

5. During that same year, Caribou, Maine, recorded 41.95 inches of rain. This amount was closest to which city listed?

_____

6. Denver, Colorado, recorded 21.50 inches of rain that year. This was exactly one-half the amount of rain that fell on one city listed. Which city?

_____

7. The year before, Chicago, Illinois, had 57.98 inches of rain. How much more rain was that than the amount shown for Chicago on the list?

_____

8. If 4.85 inches of rain fell in October in New York, was that more or less than the average amount of rain for the year on the list?

_____

9. Was the amount of rain that fell in Portland closer to the rainfall in San Francisco or Hartford?

_____

10. Which listed city was the second wettest during that year?

_____

Name _____

Date _____

WHERE DO I FIND SEAWEED?

Pretend that three pupils in your class went on a nature walk to three different places. They each took a shopping bag and came back with several objects.

   Here is a list of the various items they gathered, all mixed together. Below the list are three columns labeled: Beach, Woods, Small City Garden. Decide which items belong on each list. Not all three columns will be the same length. Some items may appear in more than one column.

> **LIST:** seaweed, rosebud, moss, piece of brick, driftwood, dried seahorse, pine cone, tomato, seed envelope, acorn, grasshopper, marigold seeds, bark, bird's nest, sand dollar, turtle eggs.

BEACH	WOODS	SMALL CITY GARDEN

Name _____

Date _____

COMPARING MATTER

Rocky road, waterfall, and *air bubble* each describe a state of matter. They describe a solid (rocky road), a liquid (waterfall), and a gas (air bubble).

Below are a list of frequently used phrases. Some describe a solid, a liquid, or a gas. Write in "S" (solid), "L" (liquid), or "G" (gas) for each. EXAMPLE: Water when frozen is a *solid (S)*, when heated it becomes a *gas (G)*, and in its normal state it is a *liquid (L)*.

sweet as sugar __S__   cold as ice _____

hard as a rock _____   pools of water _____

light as a feather _____   light as air __G__

ton of bricks _____   swift as the wind _____

thin as a rail _____   black as coal _____

white as snow _____   free as a bird _____

heavy as a rock _____   a watery soup __L__

a fast-moving stream _____   a gust of wind _____

smoke rings _____   air bubbles _____

Name _____

Date _____

THREE KINDS OF ENERGY

Energy can be changed into heat. When fuel is burned, stored energy is changed to heat. This kind of stored energy is called *chemical energy*. You have chemical energy stored in your body. When you burn up food you are using chemical energy.

Movement or friction makes things hot. Rub your hands together quickly. This energy was changed to heat. This kind of energy is called *mechanical energy*.

Electricity can be changed to heat. When electric current moves through wires the heat made this way uses *electrical energy*.

Reread the three paragraphs above. See how many of the questions below you can answer based on the three kinds of heat energy.

1. The toaster-oven uses _____*electrical*_____ energy.

2. The Bunsen burner in the science lab uses _____ energy.

3. Sandpaper immediately after use is warm because of _____ energy.

4. When going down a slide in the playground, Jane's legs burned because of _____ energy.

5. The fireplace logs produce heat through _____ energy.

6. The automatic coffee machine uses _____ energy.

7. A gas stove produces heat through _____ energy.

8. Native Americans rubbed sticks together to make a fire through _____ energy.

HOW MUCH OXYGEN?

Did you know that you use about 100 gallons of oxygen a day? Stop for a minute and listen to yourself breathe. . . . How many breaths do you think you take in one minute? Count each time you breathe in and then breathe out as one breath.

"I think I take _____ breaths in one minute." (While sitting, count the breaths you take in one minute while breathing naturally.)

"While sitting, I took _____ breaths in one minute."

"My estimate was _____ too large; _____ too small; _____ on target!"
Jog in place for one minute, and then count the number of breaths you take in the next minute.

"After jogging, I took _____ breaths in one minute."

Organize your findings by performing and recording six different activities and record the breaths per minute as soon as you finish. The first activity is listed for you.

ACTIVITY	BREATHS PER MINUTE
1. walking up a flight of steps	
2.	
3.	
4.	
5.	
6.	

Name _____

Date _____

PHYSICAL VS. CHEMICAL PROPERTIES

We are surrounded by *matter*. All matter has certain characteristics or properties. *Physical properties* tell you how matter looks, feels, sounds, smells, or tastes. A red rose describes a physical property of a rose. *Chemical properties* tell how matter acts with another substance. A rotten apple in a garbage can describes a chemical change. It describes how the apple reacts with other substances, such as bacteria, to form a chemical change.

Study these descriptions of different substances. Put a "P" in front of the descriptions of a physical property. Put a "C" in front of the description of a chemical property.

1. __P__ a blue sedan

2. __C__ a rusty nail

3. _____ a paper kite

4. _____ bread dough rising

5. _____ a bottle of soda

6. _____ a window glass

7. _____ a tarnished silver spoon

8. _____ a ringing bell

9. _____ salt on ice

10. _____ a salty pretzel

Name _____

Date _____

YOUR POWERS OF OBSERVATION I

Materials: a gallon jar or jug; water; assorted pebbles, gravel, sand, clay and soil

Procedure: Place equal amounts of the clay, soil, sand, gravel, and pebbles into the gallon jar. Add enough water to almost fill the jar. Shake carefully.

    Use another sheet of paper to record your observations. Read all seven items before you begin.

1. Predict the order in which the materials will drop or settle in the jar.
2. Which material settled first? Why?
3. Which material settled last? Why?
4. Will the temperature of the water affect the rate of deposit?
5. If you added salt water instead of tap water would it make a difference?
6. Does size and shape of the sediment affect the rate at which it settles? Why?
7. Pour out approximately one cupful of the water. Pass the sample removed through a filter paper. What do you notice?

Name _____

Date _____

CONDUCTION VS. CONVECTION

Heat travels in different ways. If you have ever put your hand on a hot pot you have felt the heat being transferred by a solid object to your hand. Heat that travels when one object touches a warm or hot object does so through *conduction*.

In *convection*, a warm liquid or gas carries heat to another place and warms the matter in that place. For example, a forced air heating system in your house uses warmed air (a gas) to warm the people in the house.

Read each of these descriptions. Decide how matter is being heated in each description. Write conduction or convection or both in the blanks. In some cases, heat will pass through conduction *and* convection. The first two are done for you.

1. _____*conduction*_____ walking on hot sand

2. _____*convection*_____ standing close to a working fireplace

3. _____ pulling hot toast out of the toaster

4. _____ riding on an electrically heated bus

5. _____ standing on a hot sidewalk

6. _____ sitting on a bench that has been in the sun

7. _____ steam rising from a manhole cover

8. _____ a fireman climbing a ladder near a burning building

9. _____ jumping into a heated swimming pool

10. _____ the Gulf of Mexico warming the mainland

Name _____

Date _____

THINKING ABOUT BUOYANCY

Materials: roll of kitchen aluminum foil; collection of washers or weights (paper clips, brads, tacks); large tub or plastic "kiddie pool" filled halfway with water; a kitchen scale.

Procedure: Shape a rectangle of foil into a boat. Test your design to see if it has the ability to float (buoyancy).

Using washers or weights, find out how many weights your boat will support before it sinks. You will be comparing your boat with those of other students.

Record your observations on another sheet of paper.

1. Weigh your aluminum boat with the weights required to sink it.
2. Whose boat held the most weight?
3. What was there about the design of the winning boat that made it hold so much more weight?
4. Who can, starting with the same size foil, create the longest boat that will float? The widest?
5. Can you keep your boat afloat with a hole *above* the water line? Below it?
6. Does adding rock salt to the water make a difference?
7. Does location of the weight on your boat make a difference?
8. Collect pictures of canoes, rowboats, rafts, sailboats, steamships, and so forth. Why are they shaped as they are?

Name _____

Date _____

YOUR POWERS OF OBSERVATION II

Materials: one dozen small opaque plastic containers with tops (plastic containers from 35mm film are good, but any small opaque container will do); collection of small items that fit easily into the containers, such as buttons, paper clips, nails, screws, marble, eraser, and the like, ending with more items than you have containers.

Procedure: Place one item in each container and cover. Pass the covered containers around the room until each pupil has opened and observed each of the twelve. This pupil then re-covers the container and passes it to another person. The teacher then collects all the containers and has the pupils make a list of all the items they can remember.

Use another sheet of paper to record your observations.

VOCABULARY

range: the difference between the smallest and greatest number
median: the middle number of a series
mode: the number appearing most frequently

---

1. Were some items easier to remember than others? Why do you think this was so?

2. What was the class average of the number of items remembered?

3. What was the range? The median? The mode?

4. Which items were most often recalled?

5. What percentage of the items did everyone name correctly?

6. Try varying the number of items and the time allowed for observation, for example, six items for ten seconds for Grade Four or twenty items for fifteen seconds for Grade Six.

7. Keep the same number of containers but vary the items and then check the results.

Name _____

Date _____

SEEING IS BELIEVING

Seeing is believing. In science, we draw conclusions from what we see. This experiment will help you see more clearly and think more carefully.

Materials: drinking glass, a can of soda, twelve raisins

Procedure: Fill the glasss with the carbonated drink. Place eight raisins in the glass.

Observations: The raisins will first sink to the bottom, rest a while, and then float to the surface. Watch them float a while, begin to move rapidly, and then slowly settle to the bottom. This rising and falling will repeat itself over and over.
  Write your observations on another sheet of paper.

1. Try this experiment with plain tap water. Does it work the same way?
2. What was different about the carbonated drink?
3. Try several carbonated drinks. Does sugar-free soda produce different results? What about club soda?
4. What caused the raisins to drop once they were floating?
5. How frequently does one raisin rise and sink? How long does it take to make the round trip?
6. Examine the remaining four raisins before dropping them into the glass. Does the size of each raisin affect the frequency of the rising and falling raisin cycle?

Name _____

Date _____

THE BERMUDA TRIANGLE MYSTERY

The Bermuda Triangle is an area of ocean off the coast of Florida. It is formed by connecting Bermuda, Puerto Rico, and Florida. Some amazing reports surround this area of 440,000 square miles of open sea.

a. Columbus recorded seeing a strange bolt of fire fall into the sea while sailing through the triangle in 1492.

b. Four American naval ships disappeared here between 1781 and 1812.

c. In 1918, the U.S.S. Cyclops sailed into the triangle and disappeared.

d. Since 1946, twenty other ships and planes disappeared upon entering the triangle.

e. In 1963, two Air Force jets disappeared. A fishing boat and a merchant-ship also vanished in the triangle that year.

Questions:

1. How do we know what Columbus saw? _____

2. Where would you go to read naval records? _____

3. What are some causes for the disappearance of a plane? _____

4. How are the unusual happenings of 1963 more baffling than what occurred in 1918?

_____

_____

5. Can you find a similar triangle of open sea on the earth's surface? **Hint:** Use a globe.

_____

_____

Name _____

Date _____

LEARNING ABOUT SAMPLING

A portable typewriter or computer keyboard can be used to record sampling. Sampling is an important science used every day. Manufacturers of consumer goods, political candidates, and government agencies are all interested in sampling.

A standard typewriter has forty-four keys. What is the probability (likelihood) that any one key will be pressed?

Procedure: Ask ten pupils to type anything they want for thirty seconds. Prepare a graph that shows the frequency of letters types. Include numbers and punctuation marks.

Activities:

1. Which letter was typed most? _____ Which letter least? _____

2. Which word was typed most often? _____

Predictions:

1. Will another sampling of ten pupils yield the same results? _____

2. Will pupils being in different grades affect the results? _____

3. Will adults produce different results? _____

Conclusions to be tested:

1. There is no difference between boys and girls in frequency of keys pressed.
2. Vowels appear more frequently than consonants.

Name _____

Date _____

LET'S EXPERIMENT WITH CHARCOAL

You can make and study crystals with this simple experiment. The questions will develop your thinking skills. Record your observations on another sheet of paper.

Materials: a glazed bowl, some coal or charcoal, one-quarter cup of water, one tablespoon of household ammonia, one-quarter cup of salt, one-quarter cup of laundry bluing and water or food color.

Procedure: Pour the solution of the above ingredients over the charcoal. Spread the partially dissolved salt evenly over the coal. The coals should be half covered.

1. Observe the growth of crystals. Note the rate of growth in different areas.
2. Compare results using glass bowls. Don't try to use aluminum trays. The chemicals will eat through the metal.
3. What differences occur when you use a brick or sponge instead of coal or charcoal?
4. Does the depth of the jar or bowl affect the results?
5. Insert wood toothpicks into the sponge or charcoal. What happens?
6. Soak toothpicks in food coloring before inserting. What happens?
7. Move bowls away from or on a warm radiator. How does this affect crystal growth?
8. What happens if you try to grow a crystal garden in a dark closet?
9. Try submerging the coals completely with the solution. What happens?
10. What happens if you use sugar instead of salt?

Name _____

Date _____

WHY DOES IT CHANGE?

Materials: apple (or other fruit), cookie, dog biscuit, slice of bread.

Procedure: Observe changes when each item has its environment changed.

1. Cut fruit in half. Place one half in plastic bag. Leave other half uncovered.
2. Pass cookie around the room. Have last child (who must first promise to clean up) drop the cookie onto the floor from chin height.
3. Leave dog biscuit out for two days. On third day place it in dish of water.
4. Soak slice of bread with water and place it on dish in paper bag for three days.

Questions:

1. What changes take place on the third day to the uncovered apple. How has the plastic bag slowed down the change?
2. Why did the cookie crumble when dropped? Does height affect the change?
3. What happened to the shape of the dog biscuit? What happened to the water in the dish?
4. Remove bread from sealed paper bag. How does it look now? How would you describe changes? What would happen if dampened bread were kept in a dark bag for two weeks?
5. Do people change? Is your best friend of two years ago your best friend today?
6. How do products change? How has your breakfast food or toothpaste changed?

9
chapter

activities for
LEARNING
COMPUTER
LITERACY

Your students live in a world surrounded by computers. While many of us have the option of becoming computer literate, students will have to do so. The following activities develop the kinds of thinking skills needed for mastery of computer literacy. This chapter is not, of course, a complete teaching unit in the use of the computer. Answer keys for every activity can be found at the end of the book.

9-1 IS THE BRAIN LIKE A COMPUTER? shows your students the similarities between microcomputers and the human brain. For slower students, you may want to give some examples of each of the four computer terms. Students engaged in the debate may need more specific instructions. Less verbal students may be asked to simply list three arguments for each side.

9-2 THE COMPUTER KEYBOARD shows a copy of the PET keyboard. however, it can easily be adapted to the TRS-80, Apple, or any other keyboard you use.

9-3 HOW IMPORTANT ARE COMPUTERS IN YOUR LIFE? is an activity that will stretch your students' imaginations.

9-4 COMPUTER HISTORY asks students to call on skills more advanced than reading comprehension. They will need to seek out implied meaning as well as literal meaning. For extra credit, you might ask students to give a report on each of the first five devices.

9-5 MAKING A FREQUENCY TABLE helps your students appreciate the study of statistics. Some students may need help in learning the meaning of the terms "tally" and "frequency."

9-6 SOME *BASIC* STATEMENTS introduces students to BASIC. This is a simple computer language for school-aged youngsters to learn.

9-7 LET'S DEVELOP A FLOW CHART shows the ordered steps of an everyday activity. A flow chart is a basic tool in computer literacy.

9-8 A COMPUTER "TASTE TEST" is given for the more advanced student who is interested in participating with his or her parents in the purchase of a home computer.

9-9 A BIT OF BYTES! asks your students to move carefully from the simple to the more complex. Your emphasis in introducing the exercises should be on finding a pattern.

151

9-10 WHAT'S THE PROBABILITY? guides students in the appreciation of the study of probability. The use of dice, coins, and playing cards gives this activity a universal appeal.

9-11 THE TRUTH ABOUT TRUTH TABLES introduces students to two symbols basic to the study of computers. The simple "and" and "or" symbols will get students started on truth tables.

Name _____

Date _____

IS THE BRAIN LIKE A COMPUTER?

Years ago people called computers "mechanical brains." There are many similarities and differences between the computer and the human brain.

Here are four computer terms compared to the human process:

COMPUTER TERM	HUMAN PROCESS
Input	Brain receives information
Process	Brain uses information in calculation
Output	Brain causes hand to write answer
Storage	Brain stores information as "memory"

Exercises: Identify each of the following as an example of either input, process, output, or storage:

1. You read a letter written by your vacationing friend. ___*input*___

2. You memorize the names of the first thirteen colonies. _____

3. You calculate how much money you spent in a candy store in one week. _____

4. You decide what to buy your mother for her birthday. _____

5. You sign your name to the birthday card. _____

6. You add up the number of cousins you have. _____

7. You write an answer on a blank sheet of paper. _____

8. You memorize a friend's phone number. _____

Group Project: Set up two teams and be prepared to debate either of these topics. Be sure to do your research first.

1. Man's power over the machine versus the machine's power over man.

2. The modern computer causes more unemployment than employment.

Name _____

Date _____

THE COMPUTER KEYBOARD

What are the special controls that we use to operate the computer?

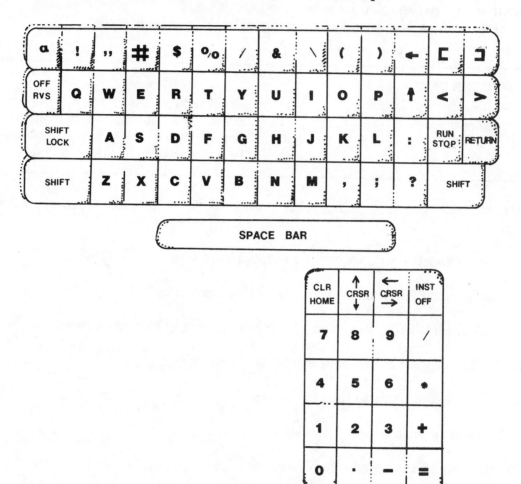

Using the computer you have available, perform the following operations and use another sheet of paper to write your answers.

1. Find the space bar on the computer keyboard. Press it once while you watch the screen. What happened?

2. Press the space bar and hold it while you count to three. What happened?

3. Find the key marked "RETURN" and press it. What happened?

4. Press the space bar once. What happened?

5. Now find the key marked "CRSR" → (right arrow). This is the cursor right key. Press it. What happened?

6. Now find the key marked "CRSR" ← (left arrow). How can you press it? (It is the same key as CRSR right.) Find the key marked "SHIFT"; there are two of them. Press the shift key and the CRSR left. What happened?

7. Find the "CRSR" down key. Press it once. What happened?

Name _____

Date _____

HOW IMPORTANT ARE COMPUTERS IN YOUR LIFE?

The answer to the question above is very important. Here are just a few of the things computers do:

a. Keep track of everything on a grocery store's shelves and make up lists of goods to be ordered.

b. Keep track of subscription information for magazines.

c. Keep track of test scores and average grades.

d. Keep track of yards rushing, fouls, and scores to predict winners in college and professional football games.

e. Keep track of records purchased to determine the top ten songs.

Assignment: Tell what job a computer might do in each of the places listed below.

1. In a school _____

_____

2. In a library _____

_____

3. In a bank _____

_____

4. In an amusement park _____

_____

5. In a television broadcasting station _____

_____

Name _____

Date _____

COMPUTER HISTORY

Here is a brief outline of the origin of the computer. Read the description of each of the eight devices.

The correct answers to each of the ten questions will require you to *think* about what you have read. You will not find the answers "word for word" in the description of the eight devices.

Write in the answer you feel is *best* described by the phrase or sentence.

Historical Facts

The *abacus* (2,600 B.C.)—after the fingers, the first calculating machine. It is still in use today.

La Pascaline (1642)—invented by Blaise Pascal. This was the first mechanical calculator. It worked using a series of gears and dials. A form of this machine can probably be found somewhere in your school.

Jacquard's Loom (1805)—Joseph Jacquard was a weaver. He was the first person to use the idea of punched cards as a way of giving a machine instructions automatically. With this system he was able to weave patterns into his cloth.

Analytical engine (1850)—conceived by Charles Babbage. It was here that the idea of a programmable machine got its start. Unfortunately, Babbage's idea never materialized because no one could make the necessary parts for his machine.

Census tabulating machine (1890)—invented by Herman Hollerith. He invented a machine for counting the population of the United States. Like Jacquard's Loom, it worked on the punch-card principle.

ENIAC (1946)—invented by John Mauchly and Presper Eckert. This machine is considered by some to be the first electronic computer. But in reality it is only a very sophisticated calculator. To work, it required about as much power as was needed to operate a locomotive.

UNIVAC (1951)—developed by John Von Neumann. This has to be considered the first true computer since it was the first machine capable of being programmed.

Microcomputer (1960s)—This machine came about because of the discovery of the integrated circuit, which is a way of miniaturizing electronic components. This resulted in a smaller, lighter machine that was capable of performing an unbelievable number of calculations in an amazingly short amount of time. The energy required to run this machine was no more than that needed to light up an electric bulb.

Questions:

1. Probably invented in the Near East or China ___*abacus*___

2. Dependent upon integrated circuits _____

3. A tabulating machine developed for the U.S. Census Bureau _____

4. Forerunner of the key punch machine _____

5. Earliest device capable of being programmed _____

6. First to have concept of a programmable machine _____

7. Added or subtracted numbers through a clever use of wheels and gears _____

8. Dependent upon hard-to-find parts _____

Name _____

Date _____

MAKING A FREQUENCY TABLE

Computer computations lean heavily on statistics. Statistics are nothing more than lists of numerical values, for example, the salaries of employees in a company or the number of pupils per class in a school. One of the first things done with a large list of numerical data is to form some sort of frequency table, which shows the number of times an individual item occurs or the number of items that fall within a given interval.

Supose the 6:00 P.M. temperatures (in Fahrenheit) for a 35-day period are as follows: 72, 78, 86, 93, 106, 107, 98, 82, 81, 77, 87, 82, 91, 94, 92, 83, 76, 78, 73, 81, 86, 92, 93, 84, 107, 99, 94, 86, 81, 77, 73, 76, 80, 88, 91

Complete this Frequency Table;

TEMPERATURE IN DEGREES	TALLY	FREQUENCY
70–75	111	3
76–80	~~1111~~ 1	6
81–85	_____	_____
86–90	_____	_____
91–95	_____	_____
96–100	_____	_____
101–105	_____	_____
106–110	_____	_____

Name _____

Date _____

SOME *BASIC* STATEMENTS

In BASIC, each instruction is given a line number. The computer will follow the instructions in numerical order of their line numbers. One BASIC instruction is PRINT. For example, the instruction 10 PRINT 9 + 4, will cause the computer to print 13 on the next line. The *line number* is indicated by Ø. Notice, we write the numerical for zero with a slash to distinguish it from the letter O. If you wanted to write a command to tell the computer to multiply 6 by 3 and print the product, you would type in PRINT 6 * 3.

Remember, the symbol for multiplication is the asterisk (*). The other symbols you need are / = Division and ↑ = raising to power.

Examples:	$2 \times 5 =$	2 * 5
	$10 \div 5 =$	10/5
	$10^2 =$	10 ↑ 2

PART 1. Following BASIC language, what would the computer print for each of these?

a. 1Ø PRINT 7 + 3 _____

b. 2Ø PRINT 7/4 _____

c. 3Ø PRINT 4 ↑ 2 _____

d. 4Ø PRINT 5 * 2 + 7 _____

e. 8Ø PRINT 2 ↑ 3 − 3 * 2 + 10/5 _____

f. 9Ø PRINT (7 − 3) * 2 + (1Ø − 4) /2 _____

PART 2. Write a BASIC statement to compute the answer to each of these:

a. $2 \times 3 + 6$ _____

b. $9 + 11 - 13$ _____

c. $6 + 12 + 5 + 6$ _____

d. 6^2 _____

e. $(6 \div 4) + (7 \times 2)$ _____

f. $3^3 + 4^2 - 12$ _____

Name _____

Date _____

LET'S DEVELOP A FLOW CHART

A flow chart is a road map or drawing of all the steps used to solve a problem. It shows the order of the steps and how each step is connected to the other steps.

A *flow chart charts* the *flow* of an activity from its start to its conclusion.

FLOW CHART SYMBOLS

start or end

instruction to do something

direction arrow ↓

Start with a list of unordered things to do.

1. Get up
2. Put on shoes
3. Go to school
4. Put on socks
5. Eat breakfast

Put the list in correct order.

1. Get up
2. Put on socks
3. Put on shoes
4. Eat breakfast
5. Go to school

Here is a flow chart showing the ordered steps previously discussed.

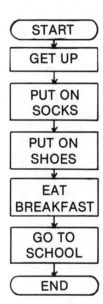

Using other sheets of paper, draw a flow chart showing the ordered steps and symbols for each of these activities:

- preparing a meal
- getting dressed
- playing a game
- creating something
- making a birthday card
- feeding the fish
- making the bed

Name _____

Date _____

A COMPUTER "TASTE TEST"

This worksheet will be used to evaluate two different brands of personal computers. You may obtain your answers by reading newspaper advertisements or magazine advertisements and by visiting stores in which the computers are sold.

INFORMATION TO BE FOUND	ANSWERS: Brand 1 Name: _____	Brand 2 Name: _____
1. Cost of basic computer (keyboard, processor) Monitor included? If extra, cost of monitor		
2. Memory size (in "K" or kilobytes) RAM (usable memory) ROM (non-usable memory) Can memory be upgraded? Cost to upgrade		
3. Color capability (yes/no) How many colors available? How many colors displayed at one time?		
4. Graphics capability (yes/no) High-resolution graphics? Special graphics commands?		
5. Peripheral devices Disk drive included? Disk drive available? Cost to add disk drive Cost of tape drive Printer available? Cost		
6. Software Type of software available Average cost of software		

Name _____

Date _____

A BIT OF BYTES!

In Morse Code we use dots and dashes as symbols. By arranging them in different sequences (.— for A, —... P or B) we get enough combinations for each letter of the alphabet.

For computer codes we use numerical digits "1" and "0." That's how we get the name digital computer. It is a two-part or *binary* code. From *binary digits*, we get the word "bit."

Most computers use combinations of eight bits called a "byte." Each byte makes one letter or numeral. The letter "a" when tapped on a keyboard may go into the computer as 01100001. The numeral "3" goes in as 10110011.

1. Let's see how many different combinations can be made with a total of eight 0's and 1's.
   First, how many variations can you make with just *one* place?

2. With *two places*, you can make four combinations. Fill in the boxes, *not* repeating any combination.

3. Now, on your own, see how many different combinations you can make with 0's and 1's carried to *three places*. Write in the total number of combinations you made.

4. Go on to *four places*. How many combinations can be made?

0   or   1   Total of 2 variations

| 0 | 1 | | 1 | 0 | | | | | | |

Total of 4 combinations

Total = _____

Total = _____

5. On another sheet of paper figure out how many combinations can be made with *five places*.

6. Do *six places*. Do you see a pattern developing?

7. Try to guess how many combinations will exist with *seven places*.

8. You won't have enough paper to actually write out all the combinations that exist with *eight places*. But, using logic you CAN figure out the total number of combinations with eight places. What is that number?

Total = _____

Total = _____

Total = _____

Total = _____

Name _____

Date _____

WHAT'S THE PROBABILITY?

Probability is the study of random experiments. If a coin is tossed in the air, then it is certain that the coin will come down, but it is not certain that it will land on "heads." If we repeat the coin toss it is "probable" that there will be an even number of "heads" and an even number of "tails" tosses.

1. Toss a die (one of a pair of dice). Observe the number that appears on top. What are the six possible numbers?

_____

2. What are the chances that an even number will occur (show on top)? An odd number?

_____

3. A pair of dice is thrown. If the two numbers appearing are different, find the probability that (a) the sum is six, (b) a one appears, (c) the sum is four or less.

   a) _____ b) _____ c) _____

4. Toss a coin three times and observe the sequence of heads (H) and tails (T) that appears. There are eight possibilities. The first two are done for you.

   HHH, HHT, _____, _____, _____, _____, _____, _____,

5. A playing card is selected at random from a deck of fifty-two cards. What are the chances it will be a spade? That it is a face card (jack, queen, king)? What are the chances you would select a spade face card?

_____

6. A pair of dice is tossed. If the sum is six, find the probability that one of the dice is a two.

_____

THE TRUTH ABOUT TRUTH TABLES

A computer may be programmed to make decisions based on whether certain statements are true or false.

Part 1. Any two statements can be combined by the word "and" to form a compound statement. We write this as p ∧ q. We read it as "p and q." Remember, p ∧ q is true only when *both* substatements are true.

Example: Miami is in Florida and 2 + 2 = 4
Miami is in Florida and 2 + 2 = 5
Miami is in Maine and 2 + 2 = 4
Miami is in Maine and 2 + 2 = 5

Only the first statement is true. Each of the other three statements is false since at least one of the substatements is false.

Part 2. Any two statements can be combined by the word "or" and form a new statement. We write this as p ∨ q. We read it as "p or q." Remember, p ∨ q is false only when *both* substatements are false.

Example: Miami is in Florida or 2 + 2 = 4
Miami is in Florida or 2 + 2 = 5
Miami is in Maine or 2 + 2 = 4
Miami is in Maine or 2 + 2 = 5

Only the last statement is false. Each of the first three statements are true since at least one of the substatements is true.

Part 3. On a separate sheet of paper, write a series of four statements that illustrate p ∧ q similar to Part 1.

Part 4. On a separate sheet of paper, write a series of four statements that illustrate p ∨ q similar to Part 2.

10 chapter

activities for
ANALYZING CONSUMER DATA

Real-life situations require the skill of analyzing data, so today's young people must learn how to be wise consumers. The following activities help your students learn how to analyze data and materials that relate to consumer concerns in their daily lives. Answer keys for every activity can be found at the end of the book.

10-1 WHAT'S ON THE MENU? asks students to figure out a food and beverage check based on a single menu. For extra credit, you might ask students to prepare a menu of their own based on local prices.

10-2 BUYING ON THE INSTALLMENT PLAN familiarizes your students with the ability of the alert consumer to save money when making a large purchase. Both cash and sale prices are introduced.

10-3 SAVING AT THE MEAT COUNTER involves meal planning and cost cutting. Question 6 encourages students to construct their own problems.

10-4 IS THERE A HIDDEN MEANING? explains propaganda techniques. Students must analyze a print advertisement to separate factual material from folksy phrases. You may want to do the first one together as a group to be sure the students know what is expected.

10-5 PLANNING A PARTY gives students an awareness of prices, practice in computation, and most of all, development of reasoning skills.

10-6 MORE COOKIES ARE NEEDED! provides students with a quick review of multiplication of fractions before they actually adjust a basic cookie recipe. Remind students that "of" means "multiply." For more able students, add a column that asks them to adjust the recipe for eighty cookies.

10-7 SHOPPING FOR GROCERIES asks students to apply what they have already learned about unit pricing. Division of decimals should be reviewed for students who need that practice.

10-8 IT'S TOO GOOD TO BE TRUE asks students to analyze a weight loss advertisement for sweeping generalizations. You may want to write the first one in before you make copies of the sheet.

10-9 WHICH IS THE BETTER BUY? includes an enrichment problem that asks students to make up their own data and then try the problems out on fellow classmates.

10-10 CALLING LONG DISTANCE I gives students practice in analyzing data. Questions 3, 4, and 5 help students make comparisons before arriving at a conclusion.

10-11 CALLING LONG DISTANCE II asks students to think through five situations and decide for themselves whether or not money is saved.

10-12 HOW MUCH INSURANCE? asks students to interpret meaning from a chart of postal service insurance rates. This is a real-life situation where your students will have to use thinking skills.

10-13 IT'S TAX TIME! introduces students to an analysis of an actual tax chart with which to tax their thinking skills.

Name _____

Date _____

WHAT'S ON THE MENU?

A smart consumer can read and order from a restaurant menu. Use this menu to help answer the questions below. Write your answers on the back of this sheet.

		MENU		
Hobo Burger		$2.75	Cheeseburger	$1.95
Double Burger		3.95	Hamburger	1.10
Fried Zucchini:	Small	.65	Salad	.50
	Large	.95	Coleslaw	.75
Onion Rings		1.25		
			Milk	.55
			Iced Tea	.60
			Shake	.95

1. How much money would you need to pay for a Hobo Burger, small zucchini, and a shake?

2. If you ordered a Double Burger, salad, and iced tea, it would cost how much more than the first order?

3. The tax is included in the price. If you gave the cashier a five-dollar bill, how much change would you get from the food ordered in Problem 1?

4. Maria has three dollars. Can she buy a cheeseburger, coleslaw, and milk?

5. Mrs. Wilson takes her two daughters out for lunch. They all order the same items: Hobo Burger, small zucchini, and iced tea. Mrs. Wilson pays for the order with a $20 bill. How much change should she get?

6. Tom and Claire have $7 to spend on lunch. Choose an order that includes one kind of hamburger, a side order, and a drink for each of them. The bill cannot go over $7.

7. Instead of ordering two small zucchini orders, two pupils decide to share one large order. The quantity is the same. How much money do they save?

8. Of a group of four friends, each switches his or her order from onion rings to large portions of zucchini. How much will they save altogether?

Name _____

Date _____

BUYING ON THE INSTALLMENT PLAN

Some consumers prefer to pay for their purchases in small weekly or monthly partial payments. Such partial payments are called installments. This usually costs more than paying for the item all at once.

1. If a car installment plan calls for $800 down and 24 payments of $200 each, what is the total cost of the used car?

   _____

2. The same car can be purchased for $5,425 cash. How much less is that than the cost of the installment plan described in Question 1?

   _____

3. Mrs. Simon bought a coat that had a price of $175 cash. The same coat could be bought for $50 down and $12 per month for one year. How much more than the cash price is this?

   _____

4. If Mrs. Simon bought the coat in October and made the first payment on October 15th, when would she make her final payment?

   _____

5. A ten-speed bicycle costs $190 when on sale. The list price is $249. If Gerry buys it on the installment plan, the costs are: $75 down and ten payments of $12.50 each. How much money can he save if he pays cash at the sale price instead of on the installment plan?

   _____

6. How much less than the list price of the bicycle is the sale price?

   _____

Name _____

Date _____

SAVING AT THE MEAT COUNTER

Study these prices before trying to answer the questions below:

London broil	$1.97 lb.	Rainbow trout	$2.49 lb.
Top round steaks	$2.17 lb.	Frozen shrimp	$5.99 lb.
Short ribs of beef	$1.89 lb.	Salmon	$4.49 lb.
Turkey wings	$ .69 lb.	Whole smelts	$ .89 lb.
Turkey breast	$1.89 lb.	Pork butt	$1.89 lb.
Turkey cutlets	$2.79 lb.	Lamb cubes	$1.99 lb.

1. Mrs. Wright chose to buy three pounds of turkey breast instead of three pounds of turkey cutlets. How much did she save?

_____

2. For a lamb stew, Mr. Falcone needs one and one half pounds of lamb cubes and $3 worth of other ingredients. His stew will feed four adults. How much will it cost per serving?

_____

3. The following week, Mr. Falcone used a pound of pork butts and $4 of other ingredients to feed four adults. What did that cost per serving?

_____

4. Mrs. Atlee needs four pounds of smelts to feed her family at one meal. A similar quantity of turkey wings would require five pounds. Which menu is more economical? By how much?

_____

5. The Hansen family prefers salmon to trout. Assuming four pounds of each fish would be needed to feed them, how much more will it cost to purchase the salmon instead of the trout?

_____

6. Make up a problem of your own using the prices of steak and short ribs. Use the back of this sheet to write your answer.

Name _____

Date _____

IS THERE A HIDDEN MEANING?

Some advertising tells facts about the product while some parts of the ad try to appeal to you through "folksy" or "plain guy" phrases rather than *facts*.

Part 1. There are five examples of these folksy phrases in the ad below. See if you can list all five.

NEED A NEW WASHING MACHINE?

The new Sud-s King Washer is on sale for $395. It is the best buy for you . . .

- uses less energy
- most popular washer in town
- made for all your wash needs
- larger power-fin agitation
- extra tough enamel cabinet

- made with *you* in mind
- cleans with cold water
- your family deserves one
- fits narrow openings
- get your clothes really clean

1. _____

2. _____

3. _____

4. _____

5. _____

Part 2. See if you can substitute five *realistic, specific* features of a good washing machine to replace the folksy claims you listed above. Do not repeat any that already appear in the ad.

1. _____

2. _____

3. _____

4. _____

5. _____

Name _____

Date _____

PLANNING A PARTY

The Snyder family is planning a party. On a shopping trip to the supermarket they note these prices:

two-liter size soda	$1.19
large bag of potato chips	$1.19
box of pretzels	$1.29
can of nuts	$2.98
package of paper cups	$1.09
box of napkins	$ .75

1. Jane Snyder feels they can get twelve drinks from one bottle of soda (two-liter size). How many bottles will they need if they figure twenty guests will have two drinks each? _____

2. If one large bag of potato chips serves five people, how much will the Snyders spend on potato chips to serve twenty people? _____

3. Mark Snyder says they will need two boxes of napkins and one package of paper cups. How much will this cost? _____

4. Jane Snyder suggests that they buy two large bags of potato chips instead of one can of nuts. How much will they save by doing this? _____

5. Pretend you are planning this party and have $20 to spend. Using these prices, prepare a shopping list. Be sure to include cups and napkins. Remember, you can't go over $20. How much change will you have? _____

Name _____

Date _____

MORE COOKIES ARE NEEDED!

A recipe is like a formula. The basic formula or recipe can be adjusted to suit the number of people you want to serve. The following recipe will make *48* butter cookes. To make more or fewer cookies, complete the table below based on this recipe. But first . . .

A Quick Review of Fractions:

$$\frac{1}{4} \text{ of } 48 = \qquad \frac{1}{4} \times \frac{48}{1} = \qquad \frac{48}{4} = 12$$

$$\frac{1}{4} \text{ of } \frac{1}{2} \qquad \frac{1}{4} \times \frac{1}{2} = \qquad \frac{1}{8}$$

$$\frac{1}{4} \text{ of } \frac{3}{4} \qquad \frac{1}{4} \times \frac{3}{4} = \qquad \frac{3}{16}$$

BUTTER COOKIES

1 cup butter	½ cup water	1 tsp. baking soda
1 cup sugar	5 cups flour	
1 cup molasses	¾ tsp. salt	

Ingredients are based on the quantity needed to make the number of cookies listed:

	12	24	36	96
Butter	⅛ cup	¼ cup		
Sugar	¼ cup			
Molasses				
Water				
Flour				
Salt				
Baking Soda				

Name _____

Date _____

SHOPPING FOR GROCERIES

Use these prices to figure out the solution to the problems below:

Solid white tuna	6 ½ oz. can	$ .99
Chunk light tuna	6 ½ oz. can	$ .79
Popular brand cola	2-liter size	$1.29
Store brand cola	2-liter size	$ .99
Well-known peanuts	6 oz.	$ .89
Store brand peanuts	12 oz.	$1.39
Famous name coffee	1 lb.	$2.49
Store brand coffee	1 lb.	$1.99
National brand bread	16 oz.	$1.10
Store brand bread	24 oz.	$ .99

Assume that taste and quality are similar or that the customer cares more about the cash saving than the quality of the item. How much money can be saved in each situation?

a. Three cans of light tuna rather than white? _____

b. Four bottles of store brand cola instead of popular brand? _____

c. Twelve ounces of peanuts with store label instead of well-known brand? _____

d. Two pounds of lower-priced coffee? _____

e. Forty-eight ounces of cheaper bread? _____

f. If these five items (a-e) made up your total shopping list, how much money would you save altogether? _____

Extra Credit: Why do you think "store brand" items can be sold for less?

_____

_____

Name _____

Date _____

IT'S TOO GOOD TO BE TRUE

The "Diet Delight" weight loss company has placed an ad in the daily newspaper. Next to a photograph of a trim young lady in a swim suit are these phrases.

- lose fifty pounds in three months
- best diet news ever
- the choice of thousands
- the way to a "new you"
- phone 706–3750 for details
- supervised by medical team

- the fastest way to a new dress size
- America's way to health and beauty
- step-by-step program
- tone up tired muscles
- less than $30 per month
- trial plan available

This ad contains five "sweeping generalizations." These are phrases that sound good but don't make a specific point. They are vague, general statements that are hard to prove or pin down. Some examples of sweeping generalizations are: the best of the bunch; deal of a lifetime; a real bargain; almost too good to be true.

Part 1. Look for the five "sweeping generalizations" in the above ad and write them here.

1. _____

2. _____

3. _____

4. _____

5. _____

Part 2. Rewrite the five generalizations in specific language that is neither vague nor sweeping. Write these on the back of this sheet.

Name _____

Date _____

WHICH IS THE BETTER BUY?

The word unit refers to "one." Sometimes store items are priced in terms of more than one. To get the unit price you must divide the total cost by the number of units being bought. This will give you the unit price. Then compare the two unit prices and choose the "better buy." Circle the best buy.

Example: Which is the better "buy"?   3 for $5 or 1 for $1.75

                                             $5 / 3 = $1.66 2/3 or $1.67

Answer: 3 for $5 is the better buy.

t-shirts	3 for $7.00	or 5 for $9.50	_____
shorts	2 for $9.98	or 3 for $14.25	_____
shoes	3 pairs for $64.05	or 4 pairs for $79.96	_____
books	5 for $29.45	or 3 for $19.74	_____
belts	4 for $3.72	or 2 for $2.58	_____
radios	2 for $59.08	or 3 for $67.56	_____
juice	15 oz. for $1.35	or 24 oz. for $1.92	_____
frozen vegetables	12 oz. for $.72	or 18 oz. for $.90	_____
cottage cheese	24 oz. for $1.44	or 16 oz. for $1.12	_____
soap powder	32 oz. for $2.24	or 20 oz. for $1.60	_____

notebooks   _____ for _____   or _____ for _____   _____

(Make up your own problem here. Try it out on a friend.)

Name _____

Date _____

CALLING LONG DISTANCE I

Rates for telephone calls are based on distance,
the time of day that you make the call, and
the length of your conversation.

Sample rates from Staten Island, N.Y., to:	Miles	DAY RATE		EVENING RATE		NIGHT RATE	
		First min.	Each add'l. min.	First min.	Each add'l. min.	First min.	Each add'l. min.
Atlanta, Ga.	722	.62	.43	.37	.26	.24	.18
Atlantic City, N.J.	90	.57	.37	.34	.23	.22	.15
Boston, Mass.	203	.58	.39	.34	.24	.23	.16
Chicago, Ill.	711	.62	.43	.37	.26	.24	.18
Detroit, Mich.	486	.62	.43	.37	.26	.24	.18
Houston, Tex.	1411	.64	.44	.38	.27	.25	.18
Los Angeles, Calif.	2452	.74	.49	.44	.30	.29	.20
Miami, Fla.	1119	.64	.44	.38	.27	.25	.18
New Orleans, La.	1143	.64	.44	.38	.27	.25	.18
Philadelphia, Pa.	71	.57	.37	.34	.23	.22	.15
Seattle, Wash.	2413	.74	.49	.44	.30	.29	.20
Washington, D.C.	198	.58	.39	.34	.24	.23	.16

The Day Rate is from 8 A.M. to 5 P.M.
The Evening Rate is from 5 P.M. to 11 P.M.
The Night Rate is from 11 P.M. to 8 A.M. *and* weekends

Read each of the following questions and write your answers on the back of this sheet.

1. Jane calls her friend in Atlanta at 4 P.M. and speaks for 10 minutes. What will such a call cost?

2. Mr. Marone calls his mother in Miami, Florida, on Sunday morning and speaks for 8 minutes. What is the cost?

3. Jay wants to call his brother who attends a college in Chicago. He plans to talk for fifteen minutes. Instead of calling at 10 P.M. he waits until 11 P.M. How much money does he save by doing this?

4. Instead of calling Washington, D.C., at 4 P.M., Mr. Stone waits until 6 P.M. If he talks for 20 minutes, how much money will he save?

5. Mrs. Markos calls Houston and talks for 10 minutes at 8 P.M. She forgets to ask about her aunt's new car and calls back at 8:15 P.M. and talks for 4 minutes. How much will both calls cost? How much less would it have cost if the first call had been 14 minutes.

6. The rates to three southern cities on the list are the same. List them according to the distance from Staten Island.

Name _____

Date _____

CALLING LONG DISTANCE II

In addition to standard telephone company long distance service there are discount phone services. These companies charge less per call but do have a monthly charge whether or not you make calls. In each case below figure out if there is any saving and how much. If there is no saving, write "none."

	LENGTH	STANDARD TELEPHONE COMPANY	BUDGETFONE
Los Angeles to Boston	5 min.	$1.60	$1.00
Dallas to Atlanta	15 min.	3.87	2.63
Denver to Baltimore	5 min.	.93	.71
Reno to Chicago	15 min.	2.63	2.12
Cincinnati to Norfolk	6 min.	2.77	2.24

Remember: There is a $10-a-month charge plus the cost of individual calls for Budgetfone service.

1. The Adams Paper Company made the five long distance calls listed above last month. Did they save any money using Budgetfone?

   _____

2. This month Adams will be making six five-minute calls from Los Angeles to Boston and six fifteen-minute calls from Dallas to Atlanta. How much money would they save using Budgetfone?

   _____

3. How much money would you have to spend on long distance calls before you saved any money using Budgetfone? (approximate answer)

   _____

4. There are two fifteen-minute phone calls listed. How much was saved by using Budgetphone on each?

   _____

   Why do you think there is such a difference?

   _____

5. Which two phone calls show a similar savings in dollars but a big difference in minutes?

   _____

Name _____

Date _____

HOW MUCH INSURANCE?

The following fees (in addition to postage) apply for articles being insured by the postal service.

VALUE	FEE	FEE IF COVERED BY OTHER INSURANCE
$0.00 to $100	$3.00	3.00
$100.01 to $200	3.30	3.30
$200.01 to $400	3.70	3.70
$400.01 to $600	4.10	4.10
$600.01 to $800	4.50	4.50
$800.01 to $1,000	4.90	4.90
$1,000.01 to $2,000	5.30	$4.90 plus $.35 per $1,000
$2,000.01 to $4,000	5.70	or fraction over first $1,000

Answer questions 1 to 4 below based on the fees being charged by the postal service.

1. How much would it cost to insure a package valued at $250? _____

2. Marty bought a gift for $179. How much would the insurance cost? _____

3. Mr. Moran sent each of two stereo speakers valued at $150 each through the mail. Each speaker went in a separate package. They were insured separately. How much less would it have cost to insure them in one package? _____

4. A jeweler wants to send a package insured for $1,600. What is the cost of insurance? _____

5. What will the fee be for these items valued at and covered by other insurance:

   a. $2,000 _____

   b. $2,900 _____

   c. $1,600 _____

   d. $1,200 _____

Name _____

Date _____

IT'S TAX TIME!

Answer the questions below using the table, which refers to single taxpayers.

IF INCOME IS OVER:	BUT NOT OVER:	THE TAX IS:	OF THE AMOUNT OVER:
$ 2,300	$ 3,400	11%	$ 2,300
3,400	4,400	$ 121 + 12%	3,400
4,400	6,500	241 + 14%	4,400
6,500	8,500	535 + 15%	6,500
8,500	10,800	835 + 16%	8,500
10,800	12,900	1,203 + 18%	10,800

1. Jim earned $6,000 last year. His tax would be $241 plus 14 percent of the amount over $4,400. What is his tax? _____

2. Mary earned $1,000 per month last year. She worked twelve months. How much tax must she pay? _____

3. Simon earned $250 per week working part time. He worked fifty weeks last year. What is his tax bill? _____

4. Carla estimated she would pay $1,500 in tax. Her earnings were $11,500. How close did her estimate come to the actual tax? _____

5. If Mrs. Hall earned $11,000, will her tax be more than $1,200? _____ If so, how much more? _____

6. Ernie earned $10,000 last year. Will his tax be more or less than $1,000? _____

11 chapter
activities for TEACHING VALUE CLARIFICATION AND GUIDANCE

How people see themselves depends on how they think about themselves and their values. The following activities, made up of a variety of guidance tools, help your students clarify their values. Answer keys for every activity can be found at the end of the book.

11-1 PROBLEM SOLVERS I asks your students to read about real-life situations and to think carefully about the solutions presented in the final sentences.

11-2 PROBLEM SOLVERS II is similar in format to activity 11-1.

11-3 FAIR PLAY! asks your students to think about applying fair play to three school-related situations.

11-4 MAKING CHOICES I asks students to make choices. Before they attempt these, review with the students the need to analyze a situation, think clearly, and reason soundly.

11-5 MAKING CHOICES II is similar in format to activity 11-4.

11-6 WE'RE ALL THE SAME reminds students that everyone has certain strengths and weaknesses. By extension, point out that many people are handicapped in certain situations. For example, a person who forgets his or her eyeglasses has trouble seeing.

11-7 REASONING FROM WITHIN is a sentence-completion activity that gives you a great deal of insight into the thinking of your students. Assure your students that you will protect their confidentiality.

11-8 THINKING ABOUT YOURSELF gives students a chance to look at themselves. Their creativity is called upon when they draw their own coat of arms. For enrichment, have students draw a coat of arms that represents the class or the school. Have them consider class activities and goals before they begin to draw.

11-9 GAMES KIDS PLAY develops your students' appreciation for rules. The trick here is that there are not sufficient rules to really play the game. See how long it takes the children to discover this.

11-10 WHAT ARE YOUR VALUES? asks your students to apply value judgments to five separate situations.

11-11 A "THOUGHTFUL" COLLAGE asks students to create a collage. Define a collage as a collection of objects combined with art on a flat surface. Use the encyclopedia to show examples of collages by Georges Braque, Pablo Picasso, and Juan Gris.

11-12 WHY DO RULES CHANGE? gives your students a fresh look at the rules of society.

11-13 A SCHOOL STRESS INVENTORY gives students a new perspective when thinking about the stress situations they face every day.

11-14 WHAT IS MOST IMPORTANT? is a more difficult activity that requires social studies skills as well as common sense on the part of your students. They are asked to think about serving on a jury, a civic responsibility.

11-15 THINKING ABOUT A CAREER CHOICE helps students focus their thinking about the world of work. It is a good springboard for follow-up lessons on career choices. Consult your librarian for books on careers.

Name _____

Date _____

PROBLEM SOLVERS I

We sometimes take steps to solve problems. Other times, we react to problems without helping to improve the situation. In each case below decide if the problem was solved or not by answering "yes" or "no."

1. Dom was angry because he got up too late to catch the bus to school. He slammed his bedroom door when going to wash. He did not speak at the breakfast table.

   _____ yes   _____ no

2. The plane was over the Pacific Ocean. The fuel tanks were empty. The crew prepared for an emergency water landing. As soon as the plane touched down, life rafts were boarded.

   _____ yes   _____ no

3. The drain in the Smith kitchen sink was stopped up. Water would not run down the drain pipe. Mrs. Smith stuck her knitting needle down the drain. The water still remained in the sink.

   _____ yes   _____ no

4. Barbara got a seat on the crowded bus. At the next stop an older woman climbed aboard. The motion of the bus caused the woman to lose her balance in the aisle. Barbara gave the woman her seat.

   _____ yes   _____ no

5. Lynn wanted to buy a present for her sister. She had no idea as to what to buy. She thumbed through a department store catalog and found the perfect gift on page 6.

   _____ yes   _____ no

Name _____

Date _____

PROBLEM SOLVERS II

We sometimes take steps to solve problems. Other times, we react to problems without helping to improve the situation. In each case below, decide if the problem was solved or not by answering "yes" or "no."

1. The Brown family had a day with nothing to do during their vacation. They read their guidebook and decided to visit South Street Seaport. They enjoyed the ships and the museum.

_____ yes   _____ no

2. The freezing weather had loosened the bricks on Mary's stoop. She nearly tripped one day while going down the steps. She hurled the loose brick behind the evergreen shrub.

_____ yes   _____ no

3. Carol wanted to send Mr. Addington a Christmas card. She knew the first name and his hometown but not his street address. She looked him up in the telephone directory.

_____ yes   _____ no

4. Frank moved last month. The postman kept delivering his mail to his old address. Frank went back to his old neighborhood every few days to get his mail.

_____ yes   _____ no

5. Mrs. Charles received the incorrect change while shopping at the supermarket. This made her very angry. She never went back to that store again.

_____ yes   _____ no

Name _____

Date _____

FAIR PLAY!

John finds a new felt tip pen on the floor near the teacher's desk. He asks the teacher, Mrs. Roldan, if the pen is hers. Which of these reasons would be your main reason for returning the pen? Number your preferences in order, 1 to 4.

_____ a. The teacher may know I have it.

_____ b. The teacher might treat me better if I return it.

_____ c. It's not my pen so why not return it?

_____ d. She may really need the pen.

For each of the situations below, *list* four possible responses. Then *number* them in the order in which you would respond.

1. During a difficult math test, your teacher is called out of the room. You are seated alongside two of the best math students in the class. It is a multiple-choice test. What would you do?

_____ a. _____

_____ b. _____

_____ c. _____

_____ d. _____

2. It's your turn to serve as a school crossing guard but you have a slight cold. It is raining, and you would like the twenty minutes extra rest. What would you do?

_____ a. _____

_____ b. _____

_____ c. _____

_____ d. _____

Name _____

Date _____

MAKING CHOICES I

Every day you are faced with making choices. To make the right choice, you must analyze the situation, think clearly, and reason soundly. In each of the following situations, carefully consider the three choices before you arrive at a decision. Then circle the letter (a, b, or c) of your decision.

1. Your teacher has sent you to the office with a note. Halfway to the office, you suddenly hear bells for a fire drill. What would you do?

   a. Take the note to the office and return quickly to your class.
   b. Wait in the hall until the fire drill is over.
   c. Tag onto the line of the nearest class.

2. Your parent wants to pick you up before 3 P.M. for an appointment with the dentist. What would you tell your parent?

   a. "Come to my classroom and ask for me."
   b. "You should go to the office first, Mom."
   c. "Save time by meeting me on the sidewalk."

3. You have brought some money to school for a very important reason to be used after 3 P.M. What would you do?

   a. Leave it in your coat pocket in the closet.
   b. Fold it carefully and tuck it inside your desk.
   c. Neither "a" nor "b." You would do something else.

4. It is raining very hard at 3 P.M. A friendly driver opens the car window and tells you to hop in, adding, "Your mother told me to take you home." What would you do?

   a. Say "thanks" and get into the car.
   b. Go back into school and tell a staff person.
   c. Ask the driver if he knows your address before you get in.

5. You are on the stairs alone when you see a squashed apple on one of the steps. What would you do?

   a. Move around it carefully so you won't slip.
   b. Nothing.
   c. Tell my teacher or the first staff member you see.

MAKING CHOICES II

Here are more situations for you to consider. Read each one carefully and then circle the letter (a, b, or c) of your decision.

1. You know that some other children in your school are going to have a fight at 3:00 P.M. What would you do?

   a. Wait until the fight starts, then try to stop it.
   b. Let them fight until one gives up.
   c. Both a and b are wrong.

2. You are by yourself in the hallway. A friendly grown-up asks you to help her find the way to another place in the building by leading the way. What would you do?

   a. Ask the person who she is.
   b. Take her to the office.
   c. Don't answer her. Go tell your teacher about her.

3. Your class line is returning from lunch when you see that the teacher is not in the room. What would you do after a while?

   a. Go back to the courtyard with other classmates.
   b. Forget about staying on line; start games in the hall.
   c. Ask the closest teacher—in a nearby room—what you should do.

4. A group of children from another class are throwing things around in the bathroom. They are also doing dangerous stunts. What would you do?

   a. Join in and have a good time..
   b. Run to the office to report it.
   c. Tell your teacher, or other staff members who are nearby.

5. You are walking with a friend in the hallway when you see a child who looks very sick, or hurt. He can hardly stand. What would you do?

   a. Tell the child to get to his class fast.
   b. Take him to get a drink at the water fountain.
   c. Stay with him and send your friend for help from the nearest staff member.

Name _____

Date _____

WE'RE ALL THE SAME

We all have some kind of handicap. It is not only important to understand your own handicaps, but also how you think about people who are different from yourself. Read each statement about handicapped or disabled people. If you disagree very much with the statement, write in a number "1." If you agree very much, write in a "6." Use the numbers in between if you have mixed feelings.

_____ 1. Disabled workers can be as successful as other workers.

_____ 2. Very few disabled persons are ashamed of their disabilities.

_____ 3. Most people feel uncomfortable when they associate with disabled people.

_____ 4. Disabled people show less enthusiasm than nondisabled people.

_____ 5. Disabled people do not become upset any more easily than nondisabled people.

_____ 6. Disabled people are often less aggressive than nondisabled people.

_____ 7. Most disabled persons get married and have children.

_____ 8. Most disabled persons do not worry any more than anyone else.

_____ 9. Employers should not be allowed to fire disabled employees.

_____ 10. Disabled people are not as happy as nondisabled people.

_____ 11. Severely disabled people are harder to get along with than those with minor disabilities.

_____ 12. Most disabled people expect special treatment.

Name _____

Date _____

REASONING FROM WITHIN

So many things that we think about affect the way we behave. Our everyday reasoning skills depend, in part, on what we think about ourselves. Think about these sentences and then finish them.

1. I like people who _____

_____

2. I am unhappy when I am around people who _____

_____

3. I am best at _____

_____

4. I am nervous when _____

_____

5. I am bored when _____

_____

6. I do best in school when _____

_____

7. I feel shy when _____

_____

8. I feel good when _____

_____

9. I would like to _____

_____

10. I like to play _____

_____

Now reread the sentences to see what kind of person you think they describe.

Name _____

Date _____

THINKING ABOUT YOURSELF

In the days of brave knights and fair ladies, families and individuals had "coats of arms." Usually on a shield, these depicted in picture form the individual's or the families' goals and achievements.

What are your goals and achievements? Think about these carefully. Then draw pictures in the sections of the shield or coat of arms below. Choose four sections or panels from among these statements:

1. Draw two objects that stand for two things you do well.
2. Draw two objects that stand for some things you would like friends to think or say about you.
3. Draw two things you would do if you had one year to live.
4. Draw what you hope will be your greatest success in life.

GAMES KIDS PLAY

See if you can play this game.

Directions: The teacher gives a twelve-inch ruler to the first pupil in the first row. She says, "We will now play the ruler game. In six minutes the game will end. The winner gets fifty points."

Activity: Play the game for six minutes. Don't ask any further questions. That's all the information there is.

1. Why is it hard to play this game? _____

   _____

2. Who in your class is most likely to win? _____

   _____

3. How would you start the game? _____

   _____

4. What does this teach you about rules? _____

   _____

5. If someone cheated, how would you handle it? _____

   _____

6. Would an umpire or rule enforcer help make the game more fair? _____

   _____

7. What kind of person should the umpire be? _____

   _____

8. What does this experience tell you about the qualifications needed by a rule-maker?

   _____

   _____

9. What does this experience tell you about the *need* for rules? _____

   _____

Name _____

Date _____

WHAT ARE YOUR VALUES?

Each of these situations requires that you think carefully about each subject before coming up with an answer. Write your answer or response on the back of this paper.

1. The City Council, a group of people chosen to govern or rule a town, has a small sum of money to spend on cleaning up the Main Street shopping area. Three different proposals have been made: buying litter baskets, placing "No Littering Signs," and hiring someone to pick up litter. Which of these do you rank as the best use of the money? Give your reasons.

2. The principal has asked you to serve on a "Clean School Committee." What suggestion would you make to have the school kept clean? Include pupils, teachers, and maintenance staff in your answer.

3. Jane's younger sister has just come home from the hospital. She had minor surgery and will be able to return to school in a week. Right now, everyone is making a big fuss over Jane's sister. Jane feels ignored. What advice would you give Jane? How should she act?

4. Jack has two older boys ask him for money while in the bathroom. He gives them a dollar, the only money he has. While he never saw these boys before, he later recognizes two boys at a school assembly as the two who took his dollar. What should Jack do?

5. Melvin needs to pass next Friday's math test if he wants to get a passing grade on his report card. As he returns to his room to get a forgotten notebook, he sees that the teacher left a copy of the test on her desk. What should he do?

Name _____

Date _____

A "THOUGHTFUL" COLLAGE

In art, a collage is a collection of objects or pieces of paper pasted on a flat surface. A collage tells a great deal about the subject or the artist who created it.

Pretend you are twenty-one years old. In the space below, make a sketch of a collage or list the details that will represent you at that age. Then, on a large sheet of drawing paper, cut and paste magazine pictures, photos, words, and so on, onto the drawing paper to make your collage. The objects shown will express your thoughts about yourself at the age of twenty-one. Remember, this is not a single picture but rather a collection of labels, objects, and sketches of many little things that add up to a whole. We call the complete collage a composition. It is "composed" of many little things that add up to the whole person: you.

Your composition is your own. You might want to include a way to show some or all of the following: what you want to be, what makes you happy, a favorite hobby or activity, the most important thing in your life, something that separates you from others.

Name _____

Date _____

WHY DO RULES CHANGE?

The rules below were part of an annual teacher's contract years ago. After you have read them, answer the questions.

---

1. I promise not to dance, dress immodestly, or behave in an unbecoming manner.
2. I promise not to become engaged or secretly marry while under contract.
3. I promise to donate my free time to Sunday School work.
4. I promise to eat carefully and keep in good health and spirits in order that I may be better able to render efficient service.
5. I promise to remember that I owe a duty to the townspeople who are paying my wages and to the school board that hired me.

Signed: _____

---

1. When do you think these rules were made? _____

2. What kind of job did this person have? _____

3. Could these rules be made today? _____ Why? _____

   Why not? _____

4. Would this contract hold up in court today? Why or why not? _____

   _____

5. What values were different from those of today when this contract was written? _____

   _____

6. How do values affect the rules and laws of society? _____

   _____

7. Using the back of this sheet, write your own five-point contract for teachers of the 1990s.

Name _____

Date _____

A SCHOOL STRESS INVENTORY

Young people as well as adults are subject to stress in their lives. The following events in the life of a young person can cause stress. They are not listed in any particular order. Your job is to rewrite the list. Place the most stressful events first. List the least stressful events last. Give each item a point value. Your first item should be worth 100 points and your last item should be 10 points. All other items will be somewhere in between.

_____ New baby in family		_____ Missed school bus
_____ Teacher absent		_____ Summer vacation ending
_____ Lost a school contest		_____ Christmas vacation beginning
_____ Failed spelling test		_____ Virus infection
_____ Death of parent		_____ Brother going to college
_____ Friend moved away		_____ Shopping for clothes
_____ Lost $5		_____ Death of a pet
_____ Parents divorced		_____ Parent loses job
_____ Sister getting married		_____ Family car stolen
_____ Change of class		_____ Elected class president
_____ Change of school		_____ Told to go on a diet
_____ Other		

Name _____

Date _____

WHAT IS MOST IMPORTANT?

Read the following story:

    Mr. Bridges is a social studies teacher who always tells his pupils how important it is to be a good citizen by voting, serving on juries, and keeping up with the news.

    Right now he is on summer vacation. He and Mrs. Bridges have planned for several years to take a trip to England. He has paid for most of the trip, which begins on August 1. He has been called for jury duty on July 15. If he serves the minimum two weeks, he will be able to make his flight on August 1.

    Mr. Bridges is being considered for the jury in a very complicated murder trial. According to a court clerk, a case like this can go on for six to eight weeks. Although Mr. Bridges is in no way prejudiced about the case, he could easily tell the lawyers that he has prejudged the guilt of the defendant and thereby be excused. Should he lie to the lawyers?

    Pretend you are Mr. Bridges. Below are several situations going through your mind. Some are very important to you; others are of little or no importance. Number your reactions, beginning with "1" as the item you would consider to be the most important, "2" as the next important, and so on. Then, discuss your reactions with your classmates.

_____ a. Telling lies makes you feel quite guilty.

_____ b. You've always wanted to serve on a jury.

_____ c. You have plans to start law school next year.

_____ d. Your wife has been ill and is looking forward to this trip.

_____ e. You will lose $1,500 in deposits if you cancel now.

_____ f. Your parents left a country where trial by jury does not exist.

_____ g. You could plead hardship and serve on a jury at some later time.

_____ h. You could stay home and your wife could go with a friend.

Name _____

Date _____

THINKING ABOUT A CAREER CHOICE

Read each of the following questions. Think about each one carefully and then write a three- or four-word response to each question on the back of this sheet.

1. How would you feel about taking a job where you were required to work with your hands?
2. How would you feel about a job where you spent all of your time outdoors?
3. How would you feel about taking a job that was uninteresting but paid very well?
4. How would you feel about working at a job that left you very little leisure time?
5. How strongly do you feel about having a job in which you are satisfied that you are doing well?
6. How would you feel about a job at which you had to make "life and death" decisions?
7. How important is it to you that other people think highly of your job?
8. How would you feel about a job in which you had very little contact with your co-workers?
9. How would you feel about a job that involved a leadership role?
10. How would you feel about moving from your home state to get the job of your dreams?
11. How strongly do you feel about taking a job where most of the time you are on your own?
12. How would you feel about a job with long-range security but no advancement?
13. How would you feel about a job that promises rapid advancement but in which you are reevaluated every six months?
14. How would you feel about taking whatever job is available in a worthwhile public service?
15. How would you feel about a job in which you were constantly required to learn new skills?
16. How would you feel about a job in which you needed to help others?

12 chapter | activities for IMPROVING TEST-TAKING SKILLS

Some students are good test-takers; others, equally bright, freeze at test time, so their test results do not reveal their true abilities. Yet, the strategies for successful test taking can be taught. The following activities help your students to develop these needed skills. Answer keys for every activity can be found at the end of the book.

12-1 MAKING COMPOUND WORDS provides students with practice in word building. The test format includes answer spaces that your students must shade in completely. This is good practice for younger children who need help in analyzing compound words as well as in handling answer sheets.

12-2 PUT THEM IN ORDER gives students five sets of four sentences arranged in random order. Students must put these sentences in logical sequence. Ask your more able students to make up two of their own sets of sentences.

12-3 FIRST THIS, THEN THAT! introduces students to the key sequencing words "next," "then," "first," and "finally."

12-4 WHICH SOUND IS DIFFERENT? reviews critical listening as an important skill. It is needed for clear comprehension of the written word.

12-5 IT'S *ALMOST* THE SAME gives children practice in choosing the word or phrase that means the same, or almost the same, as the question word. An answer column is provided to also give students practice in shading in the correct answer space.

12-6 THE KEY TO THE SENTENCE asks your students to understand key words. For better readers, have them decide which of the three types of key words each word is.

12-7 SPELLING DEMONS! uses a visual approach to spelling. Your bright students may enjoy making up additional spelling exercises with which to "test" your less able spellers.

12-8 THAT'S SILLY! asks students to do two things: underline the misused word and then write in the intended word.

12-9 WHAT'S THE LIKELIHOOD OF . . . helps students assess the likelihood of events and gives practice in handling a test format.

199

12-10 READING LARGE NUMBERS gives students needed practice in handling large numbers. For subsequent lessons, you might give an open book test using your students' social studies textbooks. Ask them to turn to a page that contains some complex numerical data, such as import/export data, a time line, or election results. Then write some comprehension questions on the chalkboard for the students to answer.

12-11 HOW ARE THEY RELATED? is a detailed activity in which your students must first identify similarities and then list them on paper. Insist that the students list at least two characteristics. Brighter students should be able to list four or more.

12-12 DON'T ASSUME makes your students focus only on the given information. This is important because many students have the tendency to go off on a tangent in search of an answer.

12-13 SAME SPELLING, DIFFERENT MEANINGS lists ten everyday words for your students. What makes these words unique is that they each have two or three very different meanings. Your students are asked to write sentences using the different meanings of each word.

Name _____

Date _____

MAKING COMPOUND WORDS

Read the first word in each numbered item below. Then read the words next to it. Find the word that can be added to the first word to make a compound word. Fill in the circle that goes with the answer you choose.

Sample: air ○ fly ○ bird ○ park ● plane

(*answer:* airplane)

1. some ○ play ○ thing ○ car ○ house
2. fire ○ red ○ fly ○ burn ○ hot
3. cow ○ milk ○ animal ○ boy ○ farm
4. down ○ up ○ there ○ town ○ place
5. any ○ boy ○ where ○ person ○ toys
6. sun ○ warm ○ yellow ○ round ○ light
7. foot ○ ball ○ body ○ five ○ toes
8. house ○ pretty ○ big ○ wife ○ old
9. head ○ hair ○ strong ○ brown ○ body
10. water ○ swim ○ fish ○ fall ○ pond

Name _____

Date _____

PUT THEM IN ORDER

On some language and reading tests you are given groups of numbered sentences. You are asked to put these sentences in the correct or logical order. Do these exercises and then make up two of your own. Write them on a separate sheet of paper. The first two in "A" are done for you.

A. __2__ Jane bought what she needed, then mixed the ingredients.

   __1__ Jane looked for a cake recipe that could be served in its own pan.

   _____ Sixty minutes later, the cake was done and ready to eat.

   _____ Then she put the pan in the oven and set the timer.

B. _____ The audience was quiet waiting to see what would happen next.

   _____ Then he said, "Abracadabra."

   _____ The magician waved his wand over the hat.

   _____ He pulled a white rabbit out of the hat.

C. _____ It shakes this rattle to warn us to stay away.

   _____ A rattlesnake is a very dangerous reptile.

   _____ It is a poisonous snake with a deadly bite.

   _____ Its tail shakes like a baby rattle.

D. _____ So, he planned his campaign a year in advance.

   _____ He wanted to convince minority groups to vote for him.

   _____ Jesse Smith knew that he could win the election.

   _____ Also, he would need the support of women's groups.

E. _____ At last, he arrived in Chicago.

   _____ First, he bought a bus ticket.

   _____ He slept during most of the four-hour trip.

   _____ John looked for a comfortable seat.

Name _____

Date _____

FIRST THIS, THEN THAT!

Some tests present you with ideas or sentences that appear in the wrong order. Your job is to put them into correct order or sequence. Words, such as, *next, then, first,* and *finally* can help you.

Write the correct sequence for these groups of sentences.

A. _____ At last, he arrived at Grandma's.

_____ First, we bought him a bus ticket.

_____ As mother waved goodbye, the driver said he'd look out for Tim.

_____ Mother helped him find a window seat.

B. _____ The suspect had no explanation.

_____ A week later, when Brown left town, the police knew he was the one.

_____ The police captain suspected Leroy Brown.

_____ He also could not explain his sudden wealth.

C. _____ The study of animals can tell us a lot about our own behavior.

_____ In conclusion, when we study animals we also learn about man.

_____ Our daily habits are keyed to the habits of other complex mammals.

_____ For example, many apes enjoy playing games.

D. _____ You could hear a pin drop as the audience waited.

_____ Then, he said the secret words.

_____ First, Mr. Wizard waved his hand over the black hat.

_____ Finally, a fluffy white rabbit appeared.

E. _____ Therefore, the noisy rattle serves as a warning to humans.

_____ Rattlesnakes can be deadly.

_____ Their bite contains poison.

_____ Their tails shake with a rattling sound.

Name _____

Date _____

WHICH SOUND IS DIFFERENT?

Some word skill tests ask you to listen to the *sounds* that certain words make. Read each word with a line under it, then read the three words alongside it. The sound with the line under it in the first word is like a *sound* in *one* of the other three words. Circle the word that has the same sound.

Sample: t<u>a</u>ble: (rain)   apple   after

1. f<u>ew</u>:   untie   unite   luck
2. w<u>i</u>de: ticket   sister   style
3. <u>sh</u>ower: rest   circle   sugar
4. s<u>a</u>t: receive   kick   catch
5. <u>j</u>ump: goose   hedge   guess
6. f<u>oo</u>d: live   shoe   laugh
7. r<u>o</u>bin: blot   slow   road
8. b<u>e</u>ll: eat   said   bead
9. <u>u</u>s: use   sure   brother
10. cl<u>ow</u>n: show   close   hour
11. h<u>o</u>me: from   soon   bowl
12. ch<u>ee</u>se: pearl   heap   chair

Name _____

Date _____

IT'S *ALMOST* THE SAME

For each numbered item below, choose the word or phrase that means the same or almost the same as the underlined word. Then, blacken the corresponding letter in the appropriate space in the answer column. Be sure to fill in the answer space completely with your pencil, and keep the pencil mark within the space. **Hint:** Think of the answer *before* you look at the words given.

Sample: to *bind*

    (a) open

    (b) border

    (c) fasten

○ ○ ●

(a) (b) (c)

1. to feel *indignant*
   - (a) sweet
   - (b) selfish
   - (c) angry
   - (d) healthy

2. a *savage* lion
   - (a) untamed
   - (b) tired
   - (c) hungry
   - (d) wise

3. to *carve* the meat
   - (a) chill
   - (b) eat
   - (c) slice
   - (d) grab

4. an *island* is
   - (a) a big lake
   - (b) land surrounded by water
   - (c) a thirsty camel
   - (d) a peninsula

5. a *fable* is
   - (a) a story with a moral
   - (b) a place for horses
   - (c) food
   - (d) a poem

6. a few apples *remain*
   - (a) are left
   - (b) fall down
   - (c) are eaten

7. the barn gave *shelter*
   - (a) money
   - (b) food
   - (c) protection

8. *strict*
   - (a) The winter frost made the ground very hard.
   - (b) The teacher was very hard with the student.
   - (c) Chris found the math test very hard.

9. *brain*
   - (a) Use your head to figure out the answer.
   - (b) He wanted to be the head of the committee.
   - (c) Leslie was at the head of the class.

ANSWER COLUMN

1. ○ ○ ○ ○
   (a) (b) (c) (d)

2. ○ ○ ○ ○
   (a) (b) (c) (d)

3. ○ ○ ○ ○
   (a) (b) (c) (d)

4. ○ ○ ○ ○
   (a) (b) (c) (d)

5. ○ ○ ○ ○
   (a) (b) (c) (d)

6. ○ ○ ○
   (a) (b) (c)

7. ○ ○ ○
   (a) (b) (c)

8. ○ ○ ○
   (a) (b) (c)

9. ○ ○ ○
   (a) (b) (c)

Name _____

Date _____

THE KEY TO THE SENTENCE

In reading comprehension test questions you must be able to focus on the key words of each sentence. These are the words that give a sentence meaning. The key-word strategy calls on the reader to underline the words that (1) name a person, place, or thing; (2) tell what that person or thing is doing; and (3) name who or what is receiving action.

For each of these sentences underline the key words.

1. The Earth's crust is broken into large pieces.

2. Sometimes moving objects change their direction.

3. Earth's gravity pulls everything toward the center of earth.

4. Cities cannot live without good transportation.

5. Jefferson wrote the basic ideas of democracy in America.

6. A bill may be introduced in either the House or the Senate.

7. The Middle Ages brought a series of troubles to Constantinople.

8. People came to the Pennsylvania colony from England, Ireland, and Germany.

9. Cities in California and Texas are among the fastest-growing in our nation.

10. Chicago is the greatest railroad city in the country.

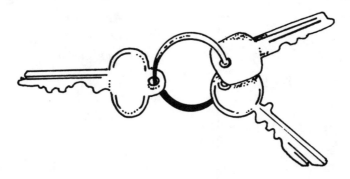

Name _____

Date _____

SPELLING DEMONS!

The words that trick pupils on tests are rarely technical or hard words. They are frequently used words that look strange when seen alone. We have screened twenty standardized tests and have come up with these spelling demons.

Supply the missing letters, *if* one or more are needed. If no letter is missing you will supply nothing for the blank space. **Hint:** Place your pencil over the blank and "see" what letter, if any, is missing.

stop___ed	emis___ion	bat___er
rebel___ion	beg___ar	wrap___ing
get___ing	quit___er	drug___ist
commit___ee	ship___ment	stand___ing
equip___ment	stun___ing	omit___ing
offer___ed	refer___ee	compel___ed
allot___ment	admit___ing	profit___ed

Name _____

Date _____

THAT'S SILLY!

Very often careless readers see on the page of the test booklet words they *think* should be there. These are different from the words the author intended. This exercise helps sharpen your ability to read accurately.

Circle the misused word in each of the following sentences. Above it, write in the intended word.

1. Climate is affected by the emotion of the earth.

2. The florist rangers wore uniforms and patrolled the national parks.

3. He needed cash, so became involved with a lone shark.

4. The lawyer's flame as a prosecutor spread throughout the city.

5. How many miles can your car go on a galleon of gas?

6. Last summer, many senior citizens felt ill because of the unusually high temperature and humility.

7. If in doubt, your manager should always be insulted.

8. The family ate franks and bins at the picnic.

9. The zebra is a horse of a different collar.

10. When the British landed, the farmers lighted deacons as a signal to the colonists.

Name _____

Date _____

WHAT'S THE LIKELIHOOD OF . . .

Each numbered item below contains three sentences telling about things that might or might not be likely to happen.

In each group of sentences, find the one that describes something you think might really happen. Fill in the circle that is in front of that sentence, being sure to fill in the outline completely.

Sample: ○ The flowers washed their petals.
● The children ate their lunch.
○ The chairs marched around the table.

1. ○ The giraffe jumped over the star.
○ The animals caught the moon.
○ The baby drank the milk and fell asleep.

2. ○ The lake waved to the children.
○ Thomas heard the butterflies laugh.
○ Nina and Joan saw the fish in the lake.

3. ○ The piano danced around the room.
○ Jenny and Laura danced to the music.
○ The bell walked into the classroom and said we could go home.

4. ○ The fish had a picnic near the lake.
○ The waves smiled at the people.
○ Danny walked along the shore with his dog.

5. ○ The kitten began to purr.
○ The kitten poured the milk into its bowl.
○ The ball of yarn smiled at the kitten and ran to it.

Name _____

Date _____

READING LARGE NUMBERS

Read the following paragraph carefully. Then circle the letter of the correct answer. Be careful! You'll be working with large numbers! **Hint:** You should know that Richmond, Queens, Brooklyn, Manhattan, and The Bronx are all parts of New York City.

Comparative figures show that the twentieth century has not eliminated nineteenth-century problems. In 1900, nearly two thirds of the city's population lived in tenement houses. A total of 2,372,079 New Yorkers lived in 82,652 tenement buildings. Manhattan had 42,700 tenements; Brooklyn, 33,771; The Bronx, 4,365; Queens, 1,398; and Richmond, 418. In the year 1978, 186,000 apartment units were still being rented in some 27,000 Old-Law Tenements throughout the city: 125,000 in Manhattan; 56,000 in Brooklyn; 4,000 in The Bronx; 2,000 in Queens; and fewer than 500 such units in Richmond.

1. In the year 1978, there were the following number of tenements in New York City:

   a. 33,771   c. 1,398

   b. 82,652   d. 27,000

2. In that year, there were many more apartment units than the number of tenement buildings. The total number of apartment units was:

   a. 418   c. 186,000

   b. 4,000   d. 2,000

3. Two thirds of the city's population lived in tenement houses in the year:

   a. 1978   c. 1979

   b. 1900   d. 1987

Name _____

Date _____

HOW ARE THEY RELATED?

Many times you are asked to detect common characteristics of different items. Sharpen your thinking skills by writing down how each set of these paired items are the same. Use the back of this sheet if you need more room to write.

Sample: apple : orange   <u>fruit, edible, round, colored, sweet, skins, seeds</u>

1. car : truck _____

_____

2. chair : table _____

_____

3. bus : train _____

_____

4. doll : teddy bear _____

_____

5. banker : baker _____

_____

6. doctor : nurse _____

_____

7. person : cat _____

_____

8. sunlight : electricity _____

_____

9. laughing : frowning _____

_____

10. automobile : submarine _____

_____

Name _____

Date _____

DON'T ASSUME

Sometimes people "read into" a statement more than what is really written. When taking a test, as well as at other times, you must not assume more facts than are actually given.

Sample: Jim won a bike in the spelling contest.

_____ a. Many people entered the spelling contest.

_____ b. Jim had never won any other contest before.

___✔___ c. The prize was a bike.

The only statement related to the underlined sentences is "c." You cannot assume that "a" and "b" are correct. Now read each group of the following statements and check off the statements that relate to the first. Be careful because there may be more than one statement that is correct!

1. The driver sent the huge car roaring into reverse.

_____ a. The car was big.

_____ b. The car went forward very rapidly.

_____ c. There were two people in the car.

2. The small piece of candy is soft but not sweet.

_____ a. The candy costs less than most others.

_____ b. The candy is not large.

_____ c. The candy has a sugary taste.

3. A fifty-story skyscraper was built on that street last year.

_____ a. It was a tall building.

_____ b. It was made of brick.

_____ c. It was an apartment house.

4. The air is filled with the scent of roses.

_____ a. It is a day in June.

_____ b. The air has a pleasant smell.

_____ c. It is not a snowy day.

Name _____

Date _____

SAME SPELLING, DIFFERENT MEANINGS

Many words have several meanings, although spelled the same way. The word *key*, for example, has three different meanings:

- She struck the wrong *key* on the piano.
- The missing book was the *key* to the mystery.
- Did you lose your house *key*?

The word *key* is spelled the same way in each sentence, but the word has a different meaning each time.

Using the back of this sheet and another piece of paper if necessary, write at least two sentences with different meanings for each of the following words. **Remember:** Words are sometimes nouns *and* verbs.

1. comic
2. court
3. die
4. exercise
5. fly

6. hang
7. interest
8. lean
9. net
10. practice

_____

_____

_____

_____

_____

_____

_____

_____

_____

_____

_____

Answer Keys

Chapter 1: Activities for Teaching Problem-Solving Skills

1-1 WHERE WOULD I FIND IT?

1. encyclopedia/almanac
2. almanac/encyclopedia
3. dictionary
4. atlas
5. almanac/encyclopedia
6. atlas
7. dictionary
8. encyclopedia/almanac
9. almanac
10. almanac
11. encyclopedia
12. encyclopedia

1-2 A SENSE OF SOLUTION

1. 4
2. 50¢
3. 30
4. 7
5. 2
6. 3
7. 4
8. 9
9. 300
10. 4

1-3 BE A DETECTIVE

At the zoo

1-4 WHICH WORD?

1. less
2. century
3. carry
4. pedestrian
5. spectacle
6. spectator
7. duplicate
8. bi-weekly
9. pediatrician (or other specialist)
10. vehicle

1-5 SOMETHING'S MISSING

a. 16, 32
b. 11, 16
c. T, F (days of week)
d. S, S (numbers)
e. 25, 36
f. 9/13, 11/16 (add 2 to numerator/add 3 to denominator)
g. CL, DC (Roman numerals)
h. M, J (months)
i. Y, U (row of typewriter keys)
j. Y, O (spectrum)

1-6 BE ON THE LOOKOUT!

1. CANADA
   PAKISTAN
   JORDAN (or SUDAN)
   ISRAEL
   HUNGARY
   DENMARK
   KENYA
   ARGENTINA
   FRANCE
   PHILIPPINES

2. Answers will vary. Here are some suggestions:

LARVA	ALIEN
NOMAD	CAMEO
CHORD	FOLIO
HAREM	IGLOO
MAXIM	CEDAR
VENOM	MAJOR
RAZOR	LIGHT
TOPAZ	WALTZ

1-7 YES OR NO

1. N
2. Y
3. N
4. Y
5. N
6. Y
7. N
8. N
9. N
10. N

1-8 THE HIDDEN INSECT

Firefly

1-9 WHAT COMES NEXT?

a. 6
b. 1560 (multiply by 2, then 3, 4, 5)
c. 18 (add 1, then add 2)
d. 37 (divide by 6, then 5, 4)
e. 36 (add 5, then subtract 8)
f. 7168 (multiply by 4, then 8)
g. 62 (add 8, then 7, 6, 5)
h. 462 (multiply by 3, then add 7, multiply by 3, add 7)
i. 89 (add 6, then 12, 18, 24)
j. 110 (add 11, then 12, 11, 12)

1-10 WATCH OUT!

1. The doctor is Mrs. Green's sister.
2. No because if the man has a widow, he is already dead.
3. All months have 28 days.
4. Yes, but it is not a holiday.
5. 49 (7 × 7 days of week = 49)
6. one hour
7. 90
8. 1.1 and 11
9. If the man is "living," he cannot be buried.
10. 36 miles

1-11 TAKE A GUESS

These are the actual answers:
1. weight × number of students in class
2. 96
3. 7 × 24 = 168   168 × 60 = 10,080
4. approximately 350 pages
5. 341
6. 95
7. 128
8. 76.80
9. $20

1-12 USING COMMON SENSE

1. three buses
2. 66
3. four
4. 12 inches
5. 28 days
6. the brunette is the blonde's mother
7. four boys and three girls
8. 9:30

1-13 MATHEMATICAL PATTERNS

a. 1,020 (× 2, + 2, × 2 . . .)
b. 2,187 (× 2 + the number)
c. 144 (× 3, + 3, ÷ 3, − 3 . . .)
d. 67 (+ 2, + 3, + 4 . . .)
e. 22 (− 6, ÷ 7, − 5, ÷ 7, − 4 . . .)
f. 131 (+ 27, − 12, + 27, − 11 . . .)
g. 612 (× 1, − 1, × 2, − 2, × 3, − 3)
h. 94 (+ 7, + 5, + 8, + 4, + 9, + 3)
i. 20 (× 10, ÷ 5, × 10, ÷ 5 . . .)

1-14 NOW YOU SEE IT . . .

1. Turn over coins 3 and 4; then 4 and 5; then 2 and 3.
2. Move coin 1 to below the bottom row between coins 8 and 9. Then move coins 7 and 10 to the left of coin 2 and to the right of coin 3.
3. Move coin 4 to touch coins 5 and 6. Move coin 5 to touch coins 1 and 2. Move coin 1 to touch coins 5 and 4.

1-15 CLUES AND CLUES

1. Norton is the aide.
   Allen is the intern.
   Isaacs is the nurse.

2. Ira Morton
   Julie Newman
   Kevin Lane

1-16 MORE CLUES

1. John is 12.
   Judy is 14.
   Mary is 13.
   Roy is 10.

2. White is first.
   Pink is second.

Green is third.
Yellow is fourth.
3. Bob likes hiking.
   Harry likes tennis.
   Ivan likes baseball.
   Tony likes ice skating.
4. The cat's name is Sally.
   The dog's name is Jack.
   The goat's name is Rita.
   The horse's name is Karl.

1-17 BE LOGICAL

1. 7 people
2. Peter/chemist/California/first floor
   Fred/baker/Pennsylvania/second floor
   Butch/architect/South Dakota/third floor
   Carl/dancer/Florida/fourth floor
   Sal/engineer/Washington/fifth floor

Chapter 2: Activities for Teaching Reading and Thinking

2-1 THAT DOESN'T BELONG!

1. circus / easel
2. utensil / stove
3. kitchen / bed
4. instrument / sign
5. fruit / onion
6. family / neighbor
7. camera / album
8. meat / fish
9. supplies / chair
10. plane / schedule
11. living room / tub
12. summer / snow

2-2 WHICH MEANING?

1. can   6. grade
2. fire   7. park
3. tire   8. blank
4. chest   9. stand
5. fall   10. chair

2-3 LISTEN CAREFULLY

Sentences will vary. However, students should write sentences using the homonyms for:
1. oar   6. die
2. plain   7. tale
3. road   8. flour
4. meat   9. son
5. know   10. mail

2-4 LET'S GO TO THE MOVIES

1. *Home on the Range*
2. *Man Across the Pacific* or *Under the Big Top*
3. *Under the Big Top*

4. $1.50
5. *Space Voyager*
6. $4
7. *Man Across the Pacific*
8. Cinema

2-5 WORD SEARCH

ail	fog	jilt
aim	form	kilt
bail	gory	milk
bilk	hilt	norm
defog	him	pry
deform	jail	
fed	jib	

2-6 READ BETWEEN THE LINES

1. not
2. toward the mountain
3. nine
4. a prize
5. late afternoon
6. took a drink of water or beverage
7. their backpacks
8. no, because their clothes were dusty

2-7 USE YOUR SENSES

1. sight
2. smell
3. hearing
4. sight
5. taste
6. touch
7. Answers will vary.

2-8 STEP ON A CRACK . . .

1. yes, plus a girl
2. yes *or* no
3. no
4. yes
5. no
6. no
7. no
8. no
9. yes
10. no

2-9 WHAT'S IT ALL ABOUT?

1. B
2. E
3. C
4. F
5. D
6. A
7. B
8. A
9. C
10. E
11. F
12. D

2-10 THE FIVE QUESTIONS

1. Bob / got up / at seven / to get ready for school
2. Judy / delivered *Evening Times* / between five and six o'clock / in Heartland Village
3. Joan / met her friends / after school / at Miller Field / to practice.

2-11 FACT, OPINION, OR BOTH?

1. F
2. O
3. F
4. C
5. O
6. O
7. O
8. F
9. C
10. O
11. C
12. F
13. O
14. O
15. F

2-12 DO YOU BELIEVE IT?

1. T
2. B
3. T
4. B
5. T
6. T
7. B
8. T
9. T
10. B

2-13 GOOD MORNING! IT'S TIME FOR BED

1. fools / food
2. dawn / dusk
3. interrupter / interpreter
4. rule / role
5. inpatient / impatient
6. moon / sun
7. clear / cloudy
8. for / from
9. thee / three
10. displeased / pleased

2-14 SCRAMBLED

1. INFECTION
2. MISFORTUNE
3. STEAMINESS
4. HUSTLER
5. WAITRESS
6. PUNISHMENT
7. VIOLENCE
8. LEGISLATION
9. FAMILIES
10. UPHOLSTER

2-15 MORE OF THOSE FIVE QUESTIONS

1. Class / took trip / Wednesday at 10 A.M. / to museum.
2. Tom / watched news / 7 o'clock / on Channel 4.
3. Maggie's mother / made meat loaf / on Thursdays / for dinner.

2-16 MORE FACTS AND OPINIONS

1. O
2. F
3. F
4. O
5. O
6. F
7. O
8. C
9. C
10. F

Chapter 3: Activities for Teaching Logical Thinking in Language Arts

3-1 LET'S CATEGORIZE

1. bear
2. wings

3. calico
4. cape
5. India
6. wasp
7. table
8. crocodile
9. symbol
10. spendthrift
11. silly
12. save

3-2 CLASSIFYING INFORMATION

1. T
2. GI
3. F
4. F
5. C
6. C
7. T
8. F
9. F, T
10. GI
11. T, GI
12. C

3-3 THIS CAUSED THAT

Column A	Column B
E	E
C	E
C	E
E	C
C	C
E	C
E	C
E	C

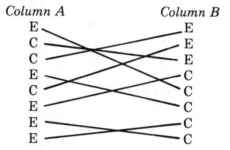

3-4 WHY?

Causes	Effect
1. sit on eggs	egg hatches
2. drunken driving	die in accidents
3. jump out of water	capture insects
4. unusual tongues	pick up smells
5. perfectly built	flying
6. wet or hungry	baby cries
7. sun's light stronger	hides moon
8. rivers	ocean water tastes salty
9. carelessness	broke his leg
10. collects stamps	for fun

3-5 IN WHICH AISLE?

meat	produce
baked goods	dairy
produce	baked goods
meat	meat
produce	baked goods
produce	dairy
produce	dairy
baked goods	baked goods
dairy	baked goods
dairy	dairy

3-6 HOW DID IT HAPPEN?

A.	B.	C.	D.
4	3	2	3
2	1	4	1
1	4	3	2
3	2	1	4

3-7 READ THE NEWSPAPER

1. B
2. 6G
3. 13D
4. F
5. 15G
6. C
7. 3E
8. 12C

3-8 WHAT ARE THE REASONS?

1. They play basketball on Christmas.
2. apartment house
3. have not missed a day of school
4. She attands every game.
5. They have many friends.

3-9 I PREDICT . . .

1. he had a flat
2. a parade
3. on a trip
4. wearing glasses
5. Answers will vary.
6. going to be late
7. chased the cat
8. some goldfish dead

3-10 WHAT MIGHT HAPPEN?

1. C
2. omit
3. B
4. B
5. B
6. omit
7. omit
8. C

3-11 OUT OF ORDER

A group of eighth graders have decided to start their own business. They plan to offer a variety of services. Some of them include babysitting and lawn mowing. They feel they need a name for their business that people will remember. A local radio station has offered them a spot announcement at 10 A.M. and another at 9 P.M. Each commercial announcement will be thirty seconds long. The commercial will feature one of the eighth graders.

3-12 NOTING SEQUENCE

Titles will vary.
1. Lake Oneonta is a great place for kids in the summer.
2. It is located just twenty miles from town.
3. There are many cottages along the shore with many children in each family.
4. The swimming is good and most people own a boat.

5. This makes it possible for them to water ski.

6. For those who don't own boats, there are boats for rent.

3-13 LOGICAL PAIRS

1. deer	9. drove
2. drake	10. chirp (or tweet)
3. plum	11. quartet
4. face	12. patient
5. feather	13. wipe (or dry)
6. clothing	14. tool
7. cub	15. blast (or explode)
8. shout	

3-14 THAT'S NOT RIGHT!

1. cause / choice
2. denied / proclaimed
3. demand / grant
4. interrupted / continued
5. measured / damaged
6. stowed / served
7. statute / salute
8. mutter / pronounce

3-15 FROM GENERAL TO SPECIFIC

2. Mary (or any other girl's name)	10. page
	11. furniture
3. table (or living room)	12. subject (or class)
4. school	13. house (or apartment building)
5. insect	
6. page	14. cat
7. row (or seat)	15. paragraph (or story)
8. country	
9. coin	16. Answers will vary.

3-16 GOOD EATING

1. c	5. b
2. c	6. a
3. d	7. d
4. a	8. b

3-17 A BOOK REPORT

1. b	4. a
2. d	5. d
3. b	6. b

3-18 IT'S THE SAME!

1. dad	mom
sis	bob
did	gag
mum	pop

tot	wow
eye	pup
pip	pep
2. Nan	Gig
Mim	Asa
Viv	Ada

3. 202, 212, 222, etc.
303, 313, 323, 333, etc.

4. 7/8/87
8/8/88
9/8/89

5. one (1991)

3-19 WALKING ON AIR

1. narrowly
2. gave away the secret
3. follow orders
4. worry about past mistakes
5. hints at without being direct
6. was blocked
7. avoid (money) problems
8. disappeared quickly

Chapter 4: Activities for Teaching Reasoning as Part of Writing

4-1 GIVE IT A TITLE
Answers will vary.

4-2 WHAT'S THE TOPIC?

E (topic sentence)
A
C
B
F
G
D
H

4-3 RIDDLES, RIDDLES

1. a rug	7. a river or a lake or an ocean
2. mustard, chili, or horseradish	
	8. a lit candle
3. a fence	9. ideal / deal
4. a star	10. orange / range
5. hunger pangs	11. narrow / arrow
6. potatoes	12. atom / Tom

4-4 WRITING A REPORT
Answers will vary.

4-5 THE RIGHT DEFINITION

A. key	C. trim
B. give	D. minor

4-6 PREPARING FOR AN INTERVIEW
Answers will vary.

4-7 WHAT WILL I BE?

Answers will vary.

4-8 ANSWERING YOUR OWN QUESTIONS

1. G   5. C
2. E   6. D
3. A   7. F
4. B

Who / person
What / thing
When / time
Where / place
Which / choice
Why / reason
How / way

4-9 KEEPING TO THE FACTS

I think the weather is a safe topic to bring up at a party. (X) I mentioned that the temperature reached 90 degrees at 1 P.M. yesterday (✓) "June is the nicest month," said Marie. (X) "Channel 3 has the best weather report" was my reply. (X)

"I like summer more than I like winter," announced Henry. (X) He just returned from a week at the shore. (✓) He told us it rained every day. (✓) He described how depressed he felt after a week of rain. (✓) I don't think weather is a safe topic to raise at parties. (X)

4-10 TELLING ENOUGH

Answers will vary.

4-11 USING GOOD TITLES

Answers will vary.

4-12 THE END!

Answers will vary.

4-13 LET'S TAKE NOTES

1. Some plants eat insects. (topic sentence)
   trap insects with leaves
   Venus flytrap leaf snaps shut
   sundew closes around insect
   pitcher plant drowns insect
2. Flamenco is one kind of Spanish music.
   (topic sentence)
   made up of dance, song, and guitar music
   started in Andalusia
   José Limón and Carmen Amaya made it popular
3. Birds are careful where they nest.
   (topic sentence)

some nests and baby birds lost during storms
most nests close to ground

4-14 IN THE BEGINNING . . .

Answers will vary.

4-15 HOW DO I DO IT?

Answers will vary.

4-16 CONDUCTING AN INTERVIEW

Answers will vary.

4-17 LET'S USE COMMON SENSE

1. Michael was told to clean the stove.
   Tricia was told to unpack the groceries.
   Bernie was told to wash the dishes.
2. Mr. A is a lawyer and a carpenter.
   Mr. J is a teacher and computer repairman.
3. Alan has dark eyes and curly brown hair.
   Felix has dark eyes and straight black hair.
   George has dark eyes and straight brown hair.
   Harry has blue eyes and curly brown hair.

Chapter 5: Activities for Evaluating Information in Social Studies

5-1 IT'S FOUND HERE!

1. index
2. world almanac
3. globe
4. *Time*
5. in an encyclopedia
6. a Spanish-English dictionary

5-2 READING A CHART

1. Delaware
2. Rhode Island
3. Delaware, Georgia, and New Jersey
4. North Carolina and Rhode Island
5. New Hampshire

5-3 UNFINISHED THOUGHTS

Answers will vary.

5-4 IN THE NINETEENTH CENTURY!

1. Indian killed white man's steers
2. Sent for Choctaw Indians
3. They did not come
4. fourth paragraph
5. Brothers—expresses equality
6. Could interpret for Choctaws

5-5 READING A MAP

1. 300 miles

2. Virginia, Connecticut and Rhode Island
3. New York, New Jersey, Pennsylvania, and Maryland
4. Virginia, North Carolina, South Carolina, and Georgia
5. Massachusetts, New Hampshire, Maine, and Rhode Island
6. 1,200 miles

5-6 EMOTIONAL LANGUAGE

handsome	health problems
highly successful	losing battle
stunned	alcohol
tired	unwilling

Students' rewritten sentences will vary.

5-7 READING GRAPHS

1. 1929
2. 12 million
3. 1929
4. 1929
5. 1931
6. 120
7. 1932
8. 150 points

5-8 THAT'S NOT RELEVANT

1. (relevant)   (not relevant)
   a, b, g, h   c, d, e, f
2. (relevant)   (not relevant)
   b, d, f, h   a, c, e, g

5-9 READING A POSTER

1. May 16, 1835
2. New Exchange, corner of St. Louis and Chartres Streets
3. leaving for Europe
4. good cook, speaks French and English, house servant, dining room servant, washes and irons
5. they did not have last names
6. Answers will vary.

5-10 STUDYING A CARTOON

1. the Colonies
2. the names of the Colonies
3. Colonies should unite as one or be destroyed
4. England would swallow up the individual colonies
5. daily because this is the Thursday edition, Number 179

5-11 LET'S DISCUSS THIS

Answers will vary.

5-12 RECOGNIZING PROPAGANDA

vicious	calm
gunman	efficient
drug-glazed	hardworking
poorly	menacing
desperate	handicapped
dangerous	drop-out

Chapter 6: Activities for Solving Math Problems with Understanding

6-1 FINDING THE MISSING NUMBER

a. 13
b. 8
c. 17
d. 6
e. 33
f. 35
g. 76
h. 18
i. 10
j. 120

6-2 EXTRA DATA

1. 33
2. 8
3. 32
4. 72
5. $28.50
6. 22¢
7. $16.40
8. $6

6-3 SOLVING TIME PROBLEMS

1. 3:15 P.M.
2. 11:45 A.M.
3. noon
4. 2:55 P.M.
5. 12:40 P.M.
6. 5:55 P.M.
7. 7:10 P.M.
8. 5:45 P.M.

6-4 MAKE AN ESTIMATE

1. 150
2. $7.50
3. 25
4. $10
5. 28
6. $9
7. 175
8. 100
9. $15
10. 170

6-5 VISITING THE SEAPORT MUSEUM

1. a. 513
   b. 521
   c. 543
2. Tuesday, 10 more
3. 1,000
4. approximately 1,800
5. 150 to 160
6. 157

6-6 EIGHT DIVIDED BY TWO IS . . .

1. 104 124 144
   108 128 148
   112 132 152
   116 136 plus these numbers
   120 140 × 2 and × 4
2. six multiples: 208, 216, 224, 232, 240, 248
3. 26
4. 24 ounces at $1.92
5. 888,888
6. 14 miles per gallon
7. $6.35
8. 10 packages

6-7 SUCH LARGE NUMBERS!

1. 352,062
2. 40,271
3. Van Buren won in 1836 and lost in 1840; Harrison lost in 1836 and won in 1840
4. 2,810,501

5. 1856
6. 768,879

6-8 USING THE INFORMATION GIVEN

1. no; yes
2. $1.80
3. $180
4. 53¢
5. 36 cookies

6-9 WHAT FACTS DO I NEED?

1. 532½ calories
2. 108 calories
3. 2,390 calories
4. Answers will vary.

6-10 ESTIMATES VS. ACTUAL ANSWERS

1. $1.34
2. $3.35
3. 67¢
4. 6
5. 234
6. 855

6-11 WHICH OPERATION DO I USE?

1. a. 32 stamps
   b. $6.40
2. 31 pupils
3. 6¢
4. 10 A.M.
5. 63¢

6-12 THE SCIENCE OF STATISTICS

1. 12 months
2. 400 days
3. 10,000 hours
4. 60 weeks
5. 105 weeks
6. 750 days
7. 26 months
8. 20,000 hours
9. 30 months
10. 160 weeks
11. 30,000 hours
12. 35,000 hours
13. 1,500 days
14. 51 months
15. 55 months
16. 250 weeks
17. 2,000 days
18. 50,000 hours
19. 350 weeks
20. 3,000 days

6-13 USE YOUR HEAD!

1. b
2. b
3. c
4. c
5. c

6-14 THE ANNUAL COUNTRY FAIR

1. 6 booths get 12 prizes and the other 6 will get 13 prizes
2. 2 booths got 8 balloons and 10 booths got 9 balloons
3. 49 per hour
4. $12.50
5. 16 whip tickets and 12 wheel tickets
6. 60¢
7. 20¢
8. 66 children

6-15 UNNECESSARY FACTS

1. 2550
2. $26 \times 24 \times 30 = 18,720$
3. The amount paid for small potatoes is missing.
4. The amounts of strawberries per plant and per basket are missing.
5. $310
6. $370.33
7. $21.72

6-16 A FRACTION OF A PROBLEM

1. 7
2. $\frac{1}{2}$
3. 15 minutes
4. Don: $\frac{1}{2}$ hour
   Jane: $\frac{1}{4}$ hour
5. $\frac{1}{3}$
6. $\frac{1}{2}$
7. $\frac{6}{8}$
8. $\frac{5}{6}$
9. $\frac{2}{5}$ $\frac{3}{7}$ $\frac{4}{9}$ $\frac{3}{8}$ $\frac{1}{5}$
10. $\frac{7}{8}$ $\frac{5}{6}$ $\frac{3}{4}$ $\frac{5}{8}$ $\frac{5}{9}$

6-17 WHICH RULE APPLIES?

a. 5
b. 2, 4
c. 2, 4, 8
d. 2, 4, 8
e. none
f. none
g. 2, 4, 8
h. 2, 4
i. 2, 4, 8
j. 2, 4, 8
k. 2, 4
l. 2, 4

6-18 SOLVING MONEY PROBLEMS

1. 22 dimes
2. 70 dimes
3. 10 dimes; 16 quarters
4. 9 dimes
5. 10 quarters
6. 50 of each coin

6-19 A + B = C

1. $13 + 13 + 13 = 39$
2. $38 + 28 + 28 + 28 = 112$
3. $89 + 9 = 98$
4. $5 + 5 + 5 = 15$

Chapter 7: Activities for Organizing Information for Retention

7-1 ON YOUR MARK . . .

1. beaver
2. snail
3. Atlanta
4. Connecticut
5. heavy
6. stove
7. drill
8. hip
9. pecan
10. hen

7-2 THE SENSES

H	F	F
F	V, H	S, T
S, H	F	S, T
V	S	V
V	H	S, F
S, T	V, H	V, F
H	H	V, F
V, H	H	V
S, V, F	V, F	V, T
V, T	H	H

7-3 IT'S ON THE HOUSE!

No answers required.

7-4 IMPORTANT FACTS

Times	southern tip
1513	Spain
sunny days	east coast
1565	Sunshine State
Places	400 miles
Florida	Key West

St. Augustine
Tallahassee

People
Ponce de León

7-5 TIMES, PLACES, PEOPLE, OBJECTS

1. 1809, Kentucky, Abraham Lincoln
2. Henry Ford, automobile
3. United States, Eleanor Roosevelt, United Nations
4. Lake Mead, Nevada, artificial lake
5. fall, larch, needles
6. Leicester, England, factories and mills
7. July, California, lettuce
8. 1868, John Logan, general, Memorial Day

7-6 PREPARING AN OUTLINE

Answers will vary.

7-7 LEARNING TO MEMORIZE

No answers required.

7-8 THE BEGINNING, MIDDLE, AND END

E	M, E
B	M, E
M	M, E
M	B, M
M, E	M, E
B	E
M, E	M, E
M, E	E

7-9 B-E-A-M

1. gold
2. tapes
3. chair
4. crawl
5. jack
6. dropper
7. price

7-10 USING CONTEXT CLUES

(1) moon
(2) different
(3) a.m.
(4) her
(5) clothing
(6) the
(7) on
(8) moon
(9) one (a)
(10) wear
(11) force
(12) keep
(13) wear
(14) head
(15) back

7-11 THE LONGEST RIVER

1. Columbia
2. 1,819 miles
3. Green, Snake, and Yellow-stone
4. Yukon
5. Ohio-Allegheny
6. Green and White
7. Wabash
8 Rio Grande

7-12 LINE FOR LINE!

TOUCH

Chapter 8: Activities for Interpreting Scientific Data

8-1 WHICH CITY?

1. Philadelphia
2. Minneapolis
3. San Francisco
4. Hartford
5. Portland
6. Hartford
7. 14.32 inches
8. less
9. Hartford
10. Chicago

8-2 WHERE DO I FIND SEAWEED?

Beach
seaweed
driftwood
dried seahorse
sand dollar
turtle eggs
bird's nest

Woods
moss
pine cone
acorn
grasshopper
bark
bird's nest
turtle eggs

Small City Garden
rosebud
brick
tomato
seed envelope
acorn
grasshopper
marigold seed
bark
bird's nest

8-3 COMPARING MATTER

S	S
S	L
S	G
S	G
S	S
S	S
S	L
L	G
G	G

8-4 THREE KINDS OF ENERGY

1. electrical
2. chemical
3. mechanical
4. mechanical
5. chemical
6. electrical
7. chemical
8. mechanical

8-5 HOW MUCH OXYGEN?

Answers will vary.

8-6 PHYSICAL VS. CHEMICAL PROPERTIES

1. P	6. P
2. C	7. C
3. P	8. P
4. C	9. C
5. C	10. P

8-7 YOUR POWERS OF OBSERVATION I

Answer will vary.

8-8 CONDUCTION VS. CONVECTION

1. conduction	6. conduction
2. convection	7. convection
3. conduction	8. convection
4. convection	9. conduction
5. conduction	10. conduction *and* convection

8-9 THINKING ABOUT BUOYANCY

Answers will vary.

8-10 YOUR POWERS OF OBSERVATION II

Answers will vary.

8-11 SEEING IS BELIEVING

Answers will vary.

8-12 THE BERMUDA TRIANGLE MYSTERY

1. through his logs
2. the library
3. a crash
4. jet planes and fishing boat also disappeared
5. Answers will vary.

8-13 LEARNING ABOUT SAMPLING

Answers will vary.

8-14 LET'S EXPERIMENT WITH CHARCOAL

Answers will vary.

8-15 WHY DOES IT CHANGE?

Answers will vary.

Chapter 9: Activities for Learning Computer Literacy

9-1 IS THE BRAIN LIKE A COMPUTER?

1. input	5. output
2. storage	6. process
3. process	7. output
4. process	8. storage

9-2 THE COMPUTER KEYBOARD

Answers will vary.

9-3 HOW IMPORTANT ARE COMPUTERS IN YOUR LIFE?

Answers will vary.

9-4 COMPUTER HISTORY

1. abacus
2. microcomputer
3. census tabulating machine
4. Jacquard's Loom
5. UNIVAC
6. Charles Babbage
7. la Pascaline
8. analytical engine

9-5 MAKING A FREQUENCY TABLE

81-85 = 7
86-90 = 5
91-95 = 8
96-100 = 2
101-105 = 0
106-110 = 3

9-6 SOME *BASIC* STATEMENTS

Part 1	Part 2
a. 10	a. 2*3+6
b. 1-3/4	b. 9+11−13
c. 16	c. 6+12+5+6
d. 17	d. 6↑2
e. 10-1/2	e. (6/4)+(7*2)
f. 11	f. 3↑3+4↑2−12

9-7 LET'S DEVELOP A FLOW CHART

Answers will vary.

9-8 A COMPUTER "TASTE TEST"

Answers will vary.

9-9 A BIT OF BYTES!

1. two variations	5. 32
2. four	6. 64
3. eight	7. 128
4. 16	8. 256

9-10 WHAT'S THE PROBABILITY?

1. 1, 2, 3, 4, 5, 6
2. 1 out of 2
3. a. 4 out of 30
   b. 10 out of 30
   c. 15 out of 30
4. HTH, HTT, THH, THT, TTH, TTT
5. 1/4 spade
   3/13 face card
   3/52 spade face card
6. 2/5

9-11 THE TRUTH ABOUT TRUTH TABLES

Answers will vary.

Chapter 10: Activities for Analyzing Consumer Data

10-1 WHAT'S ON THE MENU?

1. $4.35	3. 65¢
2. 70¢	4. no, she's short 25¢

5. $8   7. 35¢
6. Answers will vary.   8. $1.20

10-2 BUYING ON THE INSTALLMENT PLAN

1. $5,600   4. September 15
2. $175   5. $10
3. $19   6. $59

10-3 SAVING AT THE MEAT COUNTER

1. $2.70   4. turkey wings by 11¢
2. $1.50   5. $8
3. $1.47   6. Answers will vary.

10-4 IS THERE A HIDDEN MEANING?

Part 1
1. all your wash needs
2. you in mind
3. most popular
4. family deserves one
5. really clean

Part 2
Answers will vary.

10-5 PLANNING A PARTY

1. 4   4. 60¢
2. $4.76   5. Answers will vary.
3. $2.59

10-6 MORE COOKIES ARE NEEDED!

Butter: (12) ⅛ cup (24) ¼ cup (36) ⅜ cup (96) 1 cup
Sugar: (12) ¼ cup (24) ½ cup (36) ¾ cup (96) 2 cups
Molasses: (12) ¼ cup (24) ½ cup (36) ¾ cup (96) 2 cups
Water: (12) ⅛ cup (24) ¼ cup (36) ⅜ cup (96) 1 cup
Flour: (12) 1¼ cups (24) 2½ cups (36) 3¾ cups (96) 10 cups
Salt: (12) ³⁄₁₆ tsp. (24) ½ tsp. (36) ⁹⁄₁₆ tsp. (96) 1½ tsp.
Baking Soda: (12) ¼ tsp. (24) ½ tsp. (36) ¾ tsp. (96) 2 tsp.

10-7 SHOPPING FOR GROCERIES

a. 60¢   d. $1
b. $1.20   e. $1.32
c. 39¢   f. $4.51

Extra Credit: Price does not include money spent on advertising name brand.

10-8 IT'S TOO GOOD TO BE TRUE

Part 1
1. best diet news ever
2. choice of thousands
3. the way to a "new you"
4. fastest way to a new dress size
5. America's way to health

Part 2
Answers will vary.

10-9 WHICH IS THE BETTER WAY?

t-shirts: 5 for $9.50
shorts: 3 for $14.25
shoes: 4 for $79.96
books: 5 for $29.45
belts: 4 for $3.72
radios: 3 for $67.56
juice: 24 ounces for $1.92
vegetables: 18 ounces for 90¢
cheese: 24 ounces for $1.44
soap powder: 32 ounces for $2.24

10-10 CALLING LONG DISTANCE I

1. $4.49   4. $3.09
2. $1.51   5. 49¢
3. $1.25   6. Miami, New Orleans, Houston

10-11 CALLING LONG DISTANCE II

1. no   4. $1.24 and 51¢
2. 44¢   5. Reno to Chicago and Cincinnati to Norfolk
3. approximately $35

10-12 HOW MUCH INSURANCE?

1. $3.70   5. a. $5.25
2. $3.30   b. $5.70
3. $2.90   c. $5.25
4. $5.30   d. $5.25

10-13 IT'S TAX TIME!

1. $465   4. $1329 vs. $1500
2. $1419   5. $39 more
3. $1509   6. $75 more

Chapter 11: Activities for Teaching Value Clarification and Guidance

11-1 PROBLEM SOLVERS I

1. no   4. yes
2. yes   5. yes
3. no

11-2 PROBLEM SOLVERS II

1. yes   4. no
2. no   5. no
3. yes

11-3 FAIR PLAY!

Answers will vary.

11-4 MAKING CHOICES I

1. c   4. b
2. b   5. c
3. c

11-5 MAKING CHOICES II

1. c   2. b

3. c
4. c
5. c

11-6 WE'RE ALL THE SAME
Answers will vary.

11-7 REASONING FROM WITHIN
Answers will vary.

11-8 THINKING ABOUT YOURSELF
Answers will vary.

11-9 GAMES KIDS PLAY
1. There are not enough rules.
2. the first pupil
3. Explain rules first.
4. Rules are necessary.
5. Answers will vary.
6. yes
7. impartial and fair
8. A knowledge of the game is needed.
9. Rules assure fairness and total understanding.

11-10 WHAT ARE YOUR VALUES?
Answers will vary.

11-11 A "THOUGHTFUL" COLLAGE
Answers will vary.

11-12 WHY DO RULES CHANGE?
1. about 80 to 100 years ago
2. teaching
3. No, because they would violate individual rights.
4. No, because unions would fight it.
5. Answers will vary.
6. Answers will vary.
7. Answers will vary.

11-13 A SCHOOL STRESS INVENTORY
Answers will vary.

11-14 WHAT IS MOST IMPORTANT?
Answers will vary.

11-15 THINKING ABOUT A CAREER CHOICE
Answers will vary.

Chapter 12: Activities for Improving Test-Taking Skills

12-1 MAKING COMPOUND WORDS
1. thing
2. fly
3. boy
4. town
5. where
6. light
7. ball
8. wife
9. strong
10. fall

12-2 PUT THEM IN ORDER
A. 2, 1, 4, 3
B. 1, 2, 3, 4
C. 2, 3, 4, 1
D. 3, 1, 2, 4
E. 2, 4, 3, 1

12-3 FIRST THIS, THEN THAT!
A. 2, 4, 3, 1
B. 3, 1, 4, 2
C. 1, 3, 4, 2
D. 3, 2, 1, 4
E. 2, 3, 4, 1

12-4 WHICH SOUND IS DIFFERENT?
1. unite
2. style
3. sugar
4. receive
5. hedge
6. laugh
7. blot
8. said
9. brother
10. hour
11. bowl
12. heap

12-5 IT'S *ALMOST* THE SAME
1. c
2. a
3. c
4. b
5. a
6. a
7. c
8. b
9. a

12-6 THE KEY TO THE SENTENCE
1. Earth's crust, broken, pieces
2. moving objects, change, direction
3. gravity, pulls, center
4. cities, cannot live, transportation
5. Jefferson, wrote, ideas of democracy
6. bill, introduced, House or Senate
7. Middle Ages, brought troubles, Constantinople
8. people, came to Pennsylvania, England, Ireland, Germany
9. cities, fastest growing, in California and Texas
10. greatest railroad city, Chicago

12-7 SPELLING DEMONS!

p	s	t
l	g	p
t	t	g
t	(nothing)	(nothing)
(nothing)	n	t
(nothing)	(nothing)	l
(nothing)	t	t

12-8 THAT'S SILLY!
1. emotion/motion
2. florist/forest
3. lone/loan
4. flame/fame
5. galleon/gallon
6. humility/humidity

7. insulted/consulted
8. bins/beans or buns
9. choler/color
10. deacons/beacons

12-9 WHAT'S THE LIKELIHOOD OF . . .

1. The baby drank the milk and fell asleep.
2. Nina and Joan saw the fish in the lake.
3. Jenny and Laura danced to the music.
4. Danny walked along the shore with his dog.
5. The kitten began to purr.

12-10 READING LARGE NUMBERS

1. d
2. c
3. b

12-11 HOW ARE THEY RELATED?

Answers will vary. However, you should look for:
1. roads, transportation
2. furniture, legs
3. wheels, transportation
4. toys, stuffed
5. workers, needed services
6. hospital employees, healers, handle medicine
7. mammals, found in houses
8. produce light and heat
9. facial expressions, show emotions
10. movement, carry people

12-12 DON'T ASSUME

1. a   3. a
2. b   4. b, c

12-13 SAME SPELLING, DIFFERENT MEANINGS

Answers will vary. However, here are some examples:
1. He was a television comic.
   Nancy has my comic book.
2. David played on the tennis court.
   Leslie paid the fine at traffic court.
   Did he court you for a long time before he proposed marriage?
3. Instead of a pair of dice, that game uses one die.
   Did the plant die because it was over-watered?
4. The math exercise is on page 58.
   Kathy does her body-building exercise in the gym.
5. The fly landed on the windowsill.
   Did you fly to Florida?
   Mark caught the fly ball.
6. Hang your coat in the closet.
   After some practice, Jerry got the hang of it.
7. What kinds of books interest you?
   That bank paid interest of six percent on his account.
8. Did Cindy lean on the railing?
   Bobby likes lean meat.
9. The ball hit the net.
   Jennifer made a net profit of $18.
10. The boys arrived at baseball practice ten minutes late.
    Does your mother practice medicine under her married name?